# BLACKOUT

## HOW BLACK AMERICA CAN MAKE ITS SECOND
## ESCAPE FROM THE DEMOCRAT PLANTATION

## CANDACE OWENS

Threshold Editions

New York    London    Toronto    Sydney    New Delhi

Threshold Editions
An Imprint of Simon & Schuster, Inc.
1230 Avenue of the Americas
New York, NY 10020

Copyright © 2020 by Candace Owens LLC

First Threshold Editions hardcover edition September 2020

THRESHOLD EDITIONS and colophon are trademarks of Simon & Schuster, Inc.

For information about special discounts for bulk purchases,
please contact Simon & Schuster Special Sales at 1-866-506-1949
or business@simonandschuster.com.

The Simon & Schuster Speakers Bureau can bring authors to your live event. For more information, or to book an event, contact the Simon & Schuster Speakers Bureau at 1-866-248-3049 or visit our website at www.simonspeakers.com.

Interior design by Davina Mock-Maniscalco

Manufactured in the United States of America

10   9   8   7

Library of Congress Cataloging-in-Publication Data

ISBN 978-1-9821-3327-6
ISBN 978-1-9821-3329-0 (ebook)

Some names and identifying details have been changed.

*To Grandma and Granddad.*
*May my every action make you proud.*

# CONTENTS

A t a recent congressional hearing on the alleged rise of white nationalism, Candace Owens said the following:

*I am hopeful that we will come to a point where we will actually have hearings about things that matter in America, things that are a threat to America, like illegal immigration, which is a threat to Black America, like socialism, which is a threat to every single American, and I hope that we see that day. It's definitely not going to be today. Fortunately, we have Republicans that are fighting every single day, day in and day out.*

*For all of the Democrat colleagues that are hoping that this is going to work and that we're going to have a fearful Black America at the polls, if you're paying attention to this stuff that I'm paying attention to, the conversation is cracking, people are getting tired of this rhetoric, we're being told by you guys to hate people based on the color of their skin or to be fearful. We want results. We want policies. We're tired of rhetoric, and the numbers show that white supremacy and white nationalism is not a problem that is harming Black America. Let's start talking about putting fathers back in the home.*

*Let's start talking about God and religion and shrinking government, because government has destroyed Black American homes, and every single one of you know that. And I think many people should feel ashamed for what we have done and what Congress has turned into. It's* Days of Our Lives *in here, and it's embarrassing.*

Mic drop.

Incandescent. Bright. Most of all, Owens is courageous. These are just some of the adjectives that describe this young, charismatic female who happens to be black and who happens to challenge the notion that blacks should retain their near-monolithic support for the Democrat Party.

In 2008, for the first time, the percentage of eligible black voters who voted exceeded the percentage of eligible white voters who voted. This shows, despite liberal rhetoric to the contrary, that the black vote is not being "suppressed" due to racism. Barack Obama actually got a higher percentage of the white vote than John Kerry did in 2004. Donald Trump, despite allegedly using a "dog whistle" to inspire white racist voters to turn out, received a smaller percentage of the white vote than Republican presidential candidate Mitt Romney four years earlier. In 2016, Donald Trump received approximately 7 percent of the black vote.

Blacks have voted for the Democrat Party since Franklin Delano Roosevelt and the New Deal. Candace Owens dares ask, *What have blacks gotten for their loyalty to the Democrat Party?* Democrats preach and teach blacks to think and act like perpetual victims, eternally plagued by "institutional" or "structural" or "systemic" racism, never mind overwhelming evidence to the contrary. After all, this is a country that, in 2008, elected a black man for president, and in 2012, despite a tepid economy, reelected him.

CNN analyst Van Jones attributed Trump's victory in

2016 to "whitelash." On election night, Jones explained: "This was a whitelash against a changing country. It was whitelash against a black president in part. And that's the part where the pain comes." But where is the evidence? Of 700 counties that voted for Obama in 2008 and 2012, 200 switched to Trump in 2016. When were the white voters in those counties bitten by the racist radioactive spider? The city with more than 100,000 in population that voted most for Trump was Abilene, Texas. Yet this majority-white city, founded in 1881, recently overwhelmingly voted for its first black mayor.

The biggest problem in the black community is not racism, inequality, lack of access to health care, climate change, the alleged need for "commonsense gun control laws," or any of number of the arguments Democrats pitch to blacks to secure that 90-percent-plus black vote. The number one problem in the black community, as Owens told Congress, is a lack of fathers in the home.

Economist Walter Williams points out that the percentage of blacks born outside of wedlock in 1940 was approximately 12 percent. In 1965, when Daniel Patrick Moynihan published a report called "The Negro Family: A Case For National Action," the percentage of black children entering the world without a father in the house was at 25 percent.

Moynihan warned about the dysfunction created by absentee fathers, including a greater likelihood of kids dropping out of school, an increased probability that kids would end up in poverty, and a greater likelihood that such children would commit crime and end up incarcerated. In a speech on Father's Day in 2008, then-senator Barack Obama said: "We know that more than half of all black children live in single-parent households, a number that has doubled—doubled—since we were children. We know the statistics—that children who grow up without a father are five times more likely to live in poverty and commit crime; nine times more likely to drop out of schools, and twenty times more likely to end up in prison. They are more likely to have behavioral problems, or run away from home, or become teenage parents themselves. And the foundations of our community are weaker because of it."

Today, according to the Centers for Disease Control and Prevention, nearly 70 percent of black children enter into the world without a father in the household. At the congressional hearing on white nationalism, Owens said, "If we're going to have a hearing on white supremacy, we are assuming that the biggest victims of that are minority Americans. And presumably this hearing would be to stop that and preserve the lives of minority Americans. Which, based on the hierarchy of what's impacting minority Americans, if I had to make a list of one hundred things, white nationalism would not make the list."

Eric Holder, President Barack Obama's first attorney general, denounced what he called "pernicious racism." At a commencement speech before a historically black college, Holder said, "Nor does the greatest threat to equal opportunity any longer reside in overtly discriminatory statutes like the 'separate but equal' laws of sixty years ago. Since the era of *Brown [v. Board of Education]*, laws making classifications based on race have been subjected to a legal standard known as 'strict scrutiny.' Almost invariably, these statutes, when tested, fail to pass constitutional muster. But there are policies that too easily escape such scrutiny because they have the appearance of being race-neutral. Their impacts, however, are anything but. This is the concern we must contend with today: policies that impede equal opportunity in fact, if not in form."

Yet about the current state of anti-black racism in America, Holder's future boss, then-senator Obama, said something different. In a speech at a historically black college, Obama saluted what he called the "Moses generation," the generation of Martin Luther King. Obama said, "The Moses generation has gotten us 90 percent of the way there.

It is up to my generation, the Joshua generation, to get us the additional 10 percent." Again, this was before he was elected and reelected as the first black president of the United States. One can assume that Obama's milestone election whittled down that remaining 10 percent.

In 1997, a *Time*/CNN poll asked black and white teens whether racism is a major problem in America. Not too surprisingly, a majority of both black and white teens said yes. But then black teens were asked whether racism was a "big problem," a "small problem," or "no problem at all" in their own daily lives. Eighty-nine percent of black teens said that racism was a small problem or no problem at all in their own daily lives. In fact, more black teens than white teens called "failure to take advantage of available opportunities" a bigger problem than racism.

Today, however bad-off someone black might be, whatever he or she is going through is nothing like the obstacle course black men and women dealt with two generations ago. For today's generation of blacks to act as if their struggle compares to that of two generations ago insults and diminishes that generation's struggle.

Reparations are the latest shiny object dangled to entice black voters. Several of the 2020 Democrat presidential candidates support establishing a commission to study it. But the problem is simple. Reparations are the extraction of money from people who were never slave owners to be given to people who were never slaves. It is revenge for something that was done to ancestors at the expense of people who had nothing to do with it.

Older black people went through a lot. Accordingly, they have understandable and well-deserved hard memories. It is within the living memory of blacks that endured Jim Crow. When I was born, Jackie Robinson had broken the modern baseball color barrier just a few years earlier. When I was born, interracial marriage was still illegal in several states.

But of the post–civil rights era blacks, the well-dressed tenured-professor types one sees on CNN and MSNBC, what was *their* struggle? Microaggressions? He or she was followed in a department store? Someone mistook him or her for a store clerk? Oh, the humanity!

The number one cause of preventable death for young white men is accidents, like car accidents. The number one cause of death, preventable and unpreventable, for young black men is homicide, and almost always at the hands of another black man. There are approximately 500,000 non-homicide violent interracial felony crimes committed every year in recent years. According to the FBI, nearly 90 percent of the cases are black perpetrator/white victim, with just 10 percent white perpetrator/black victim. Where is the congressional hearing on this?

Dean Baquet, executive editor of the *New York Times*, once admitted: "The left, as a rule, does not want to hear thoughtful disagreement." The black Left is worse. It does not feel thoughtful disagreement even exists. Owens, for example, was called, believe it or not, "a white supremacist"!

Where is the thoughtful discussion about the fact that nearly one-third of abortions are performed on black women; that illegal immigration disproportionately hurts unskilled blacks; that the welfare state has incentivized women to marry the government and men to abandon their financial and moral responsibility; that the demonization of the police causes them to pull back, resulting in an increase of crime, the victims of which are disproportionately black; the lack of choice in education especially harms urban blacks; and that programs like race-based preferences for college admission and the Community Reinvestment Act are hurting more than helping?

Recent polls show that blacks, thanks in part to people like Owens, are beginning to rethink their devotion to the Democrat Party. Some polls in late 2019 found black support for President Trump at more than 30 percent. Even an

NAACP poll put black Trump approval at 21 percent, nearly three times the percentage of the black vote Trump received in 2016.

More than thirty years ago, Harvard sociologist Orlando Patterson, a black Democrat, said, "The sociological truths are that America, while still flawed in its race relations . . . is now the least racist white-majority society in the world; has a better record of legal protection of minorities than any other society, white or black; offers more opportunities to a greater number of black persons than any other society, including all those of Africa."

Carry on, Ms. Owens.

—Larry Elder, January 2020

# WHAT DO YOU HAVE TO LOSE?

What does it mean today to be a black American? Does it even mean anything more than simply my skin color being black and my having been born in a landmass bordering the Atlantic and Pacific Oceans? Indeed, why does being a black Canadian, a black Russian, or just even a black person from southern Africa not carry quite the same weight as being a black *American* does? Why has my identity group been debated with more significance than those in other countries of the world?

If you are a black person in America today, your identity is as much defined by your skin color as it was more than a hundred years ago and quite similarly, for all the wrong reasons.

To be a black American means to have your life narrative predetermined: a routine of failure followed by alleged blamelessness due to perceived impotence. It means constant subjection to the bigotry of lowered expectations, a culture of pacifying our shortcomings through predisposition.

Above all else, being black in America today means to sit at the epicenter of the struggle for the soul of our nation, a vital struggle that will come to define the future of not only our community, but our country. A struggle between victimhood and victorhood, and which adoption will bring forth prosperity.

Will we decide upon victimhood? Will we choose to absolve ourselves of personal responsibility and simply accept welfare and handouts from the state? Or will we awaken ourselves to our potential through the recognition of our own culpability?

It is undeniable that for black America, the Democrats have had the upper hand for several decades. They have expertly manipulated our emotions, commanding the unquestionable commitment of our votes. Unlike the physical enslavement of our ancestors' past, today the bondage is mental. Our compulsive voting patterns empower no one but the Democrat leaders themselves, yet we remain invested in their promise that welfarism, economic egalitarianism, and socialism will somehow render us freer.

Understand that it was not always like this. While blacks certainly have always generally voted in a bloc, that bloc did not always exist beneath the Democrat Party. In the beginning, of course, blacks were committed Republicans. When black men were given the right to vote in the 1870s, they cast their ballots on behalf of the party of their great emancipator, Abraham Lincoln. Post–Civil War Reconstruction efforts began strong—blacks were given land to work and federal protection courtesy of Union soldiers, and in short time went into business and were elected to political offices. But southern Democrats, still wallowing in their defeat from the Civil War, were outraged to see that the formerly enslaved were ascending in social status, and would soon avenge their grievances.

Buoyed by the 1865 assassination of Abraham Lincoln and the resultant presidential appointment of his vice president, Democrat Andrew Johnson, southern Democrats began efforts to reverse every Reconstructionist gain. White vigilante bands used physical force to keep blacks from voting, allowing for segregationists to be elected to Congress. With their political power affirmed, new regulations, which would come to be known as "Jim Crow laws," were implemented. Stripping blacks of their newly gained sense of enfranchisement, these laws redesignated blacks as second-class citizens. Then came the Compromise of 1877: After a corrupted presidential election of 1876, Democrats agreed to concede to Republican candidate Rutherford Hayes—on the condition of his agreement to remove Union troops from the South. After the Civil War, Union troops were stationed throughout southern states to, among other things, safeguard the newfound rights of black Americans. The compromise left black Americans once again at the full mercy of racist whites, who were determined to be restored to their prewar lifestyles. Naturally, after so many demeaning blows delivered at the hands of Democrats, blacks remained fiercely loyal to the Republican Party. So when did this begin to change?

Fifty years later, when the nation was engulfed by the Great Depression, a Democrat's promise of government programs that would lift *every* American out caught the attention of struggling black citizens. In March 1936, eight months before the presidential election pitting Franklin Delano Roosevelt against Republican Alf Landon, Kelly Miller of the *Pittsburgh Courier* (one of the most widely read black newspapers in the country) explained why he believed blacks should keep Roosevelt in the White House. He wrote,

*I am for the re-election of Roosevelt because his admin-
istration has done as much for the benefit of the Negro
as could have humanly been expected under all of the
handicapping circumstances with which he had to contend. There has been no hint or squint in the direction
of hostile and unfriendly racial legislation. Scarcely a
harsh denunciatory word has been heard in the Halls
of Congress against the Negro, such as we had become
accustomed to for a generation under both Democratic
and Republican rule. Roosevelt has given the Negro
larger recognition by way of appointive positions than
any other administration, Democratic or Republican,
since Theodore Roosevelt. In the administration of huge
appropriations for work and relief, the Negro has shared
according to his needs. . . .*

While the New Deal was far from perfect and FDR
stopped short of actively advocating for black civil rights,
his efforts were deemed more substantive than his opposing
Republican contender. Blacks saw a window of opportunity
and they took it, with a decisive 71 percent of them casting
their ballot on behalf of the Democrat nominee. Through
the lens of their subhuman treatment and economic desper-
ation, they felt that they had nothing to lose.

Then, thirty years later, Democrat president Lyndon B. Johnson signed both the Civil Rights Act of 1964 and the Voting Rights Act of 1965 into law, all but cementing his party's stranglehold on the black vote for decades to come. It was a watershed moment in American history—a pledged breakthrough for the black community. At long last, blacks would be able to bid farewell to the days of oppression, and step fully inside the American dream.

Of course, no such thing happened, or else I would have no need to write this book. In reality, despite our faithful marriage to the Democrat Party, black America has made scarcely any improvement by way of closing the achievement gap with white Americans.

A 2018 study by the Economic Policy Institute was commissioned as a follow-up to a similar study conducted some fifty years earlier. The results offered insight into the condition of black America today, compared to the black America of Lyndon B. Johnson's time:

1) African Americans today are much better educated than they were in 1968 but still lag behind whites in overall educational attainment.

2) African Americans are 2.5 times as likely to be in poverty as whites, and the median white family has almost 10 times as much wealth as the median black family.

3) With respect to homeownership, unemployment, and incarceration, conditions for black Americans have either failed to improve relative to whites or have worsened.

4) In 2017 the black unemployment rate was 7.5 percent, up from 6.7 percent in 1968, and is still roughly twice the white unemployment rate.

5) In 2015, the black homeownership rate was just over 40 percent, virtually unchanged since 1968, and trailing a full 30 points behind the white homeownership rate, which saw modest gains over the same period.

6) The share of African Americans in prison or jail almost tripled between 1968 and 2016 and is

currently more than six times the white incarceration rate.

In short, despite overwhelmingly casting our votes for Democrat political candidates, disparities between white Americans and black Americans still exist and across many categories have worsened. Certainly no sane person would make the argument that America has become a more racist country since the 1960s, which gives way to the obvious truth that these disparities have little do with systemic oppressions. But obvious truths have never been the way of the Democrat Party.

Like FDR and LBJ before them, today's Democrat leaders establish their bases by theatrically harping on the struggles of minorities. They lament the injustice of our circumstances, with an all-too-familiar silver-lined promise that a *vote for them* will surely turn things around. Of course, the success of this repeat broken-promise strategy is fueled by our acceptance of their victim narrative. And because victims cannot also be victors, the end result is a paradoxical nightmare: an endless cycle of voting for necessary change, while refusing to change the way in which we vote, necessarily.

"What the hell do you have to lose?" Donald Trump's words were direct and precise, and as I watched him from my television screen in his August 19, 2016, campaign stop in Dimondale, Michigan, I could not help but nod in agreement. He was emphatic as he implored blacks to consider voting for him in the upcoming presidential election. "You're living in poverty; your schools are no good," he said. "You have no jobs; 58 percent of your youth is unemployed."

In his blunt, matter-of-fact way, Trump called attention to a reality that had gone unspoken for far too long: While Democrats have long acknowledged our struggles and the crimes enacted against us, they have done little to provide actual remedies or prepare us for a future that does not center on our brokenness. Trump's speech was a call to action for anyone who dared to abandon the status quo in favor of real change. This moment—Trump's simple question— forever altered me. I instantly felt a tide of urgency, because deep down I knew the answer to his question. Deep down we all know the answer to his question.

We now know that Trump was, indeed, elected as the forty-fifth president of the United States, just as we also know that the majority of the black vote went to his Democrat opponent, Hillary Clinton. What has transpired since then has been a social fracturing like nothing we have ever seen in this country. Hard lines have been drawn in the sand, and blacks have, predictably, stood on the left side of them, but as we approach the 2020 election, I am asking the black community—I am asking you, reader—to consider the realities of our current economic state, the condition of our schools and neighborhoods, the number of our young men who are incarcerated.

The Democrat Party teaches that more law, more government, more state is the answer—but they are wrong. We cannot rely upon a hopelessly inefficient and burdensome government to fix what we ourselves refuse to do.

My challenge to every American is simple: reject the Left's victim narrative and do it yourself. Because we will never realize the true potential that this incredible country has to offer—in the land of the free and the home of the brave—if we continue to be shackled by the great myth of government deliverance.

Throughout the rest of this book, I will detail just why I believe the Democrat Party's policies have led to the erosion of the black community by fostering a persistent victim mentality. I will explain how a radicalized push for feminism is both emasculating and criminalizing men who are needed to lead strong families, and I will reveal the fallacy of socialism, in its inherent argument for the very same government that crippled black America in the first place. Lastly, I will expose the inefficiency of the left-leaning public education system and tackle the media's role in the collective brainwashing of our youth.

And then I will ask again: What do you have to lose?

Because I believe the answer is *everything*, if we do not **blackout** from this toxic, illiberal, progressive agenda, which has precipitated little more than helplessness.

# 1

## ON CONSERVATISM

There has been a lot of conjecture about how I became the person I am today—why I believe what I believe, what drives the energy that so deeply commits me to the truth. The answer is and will forever be my grandparents.

I was nine years old when my paternal grandfather showed up at my childhood home and upended my life as I knew it. Up to that point, it was the custom for my three siblings and me to visit my grandparents' home on the weekends. They lived in a middle-class neighborhood in Stamford, Connecticut, in a home that was well-kept and comfortable. We loved our weekend visits because they had a yard that we could run around and play in, and where my grandfather could teach us to ride bikes down their long driveway. It was nothing like our home. As a family of six, we lived across town in a small, three-bedroom apartment within a run-down, roach-infested building.

Living among a cluster of impoverished residents meant that fistfights, police visits, and drama were commonplace. I am told that this is what inspired my grandparents to insist that our entire family move in with them—a fear that their offspring might become that of their surroundings. And so in short order, we were whisked away from the instability of our neighborhood into an environment that would more properly fertilize our futures. In retrospect, this move across town was one of the greatest blessings of my life. It gave me my first real chance to choose something different. I didn't know it at the time but it would come to represent my earliest introduction to conservatism.

## PLANTING THE SEEDS OF CONSERVATISM

My grandfather was born in 1941 on a sharecropping farm in Fayetteville, North Carolina. Born into the segregated life of the Jim Crow South, his childhood was shaped by work and routine. He took on his first responsibilities when he was just five years old. It was his task to lay the farm's tobacco out to dry in an attic. He tells me today that he would complete this task at the crack of dawn, before the blistering Carolina sun could make the prospect unbearable. He was one of twelve children, and everyone had a job to do.

His father, my great-grandfather, was a notorious philanderer who would leave his wife and children intermittently, to live with his mistresses. His actions placed a further strain on his family financially, and pressure on his many sons, to step up and take responsibility. The burden forced my grandfather to become a man at a young age. In one instance, still just a young teenager himself, my grandfather decided to show up at the home of his father's mistress. He there confronted his father, telling him that he needed to return home to his family, and take care of his responsibility.

Watching his mother and siblings suffer from the dishonorable behavior of a man formed immutable elements of my grandfather's character. He made the decision then that when the time came, he would become the man his father never was; one day, he would prioritize his family above all else. And indeed he would.

It is necessary to know who my grandfather was in his

day to understand who I am in mine. In the prism of our genetics, I am the light refraction of my grandfather's spirit. My character, my work ethic, even my stubborn nature, are so closely embedded in him.

There is no doubt that my grandfather experienced *real* racism in his childhood. In the 1940s segregated South, the domestic terrorism of Democrat Ku Klux Klansmen was part and parcel of the black American life. I should pause here to explain why I refer to them as the Democrats' Klansmen, since in the elaborate rewriting of their own history, their party has attempted to dissociate themselves from the Ku Klux Klan.

In the spring of 1866, just one year after the Civil War, a group of six Confederate war veterans met in the law office of Judge M. Thomas Jones and began the Ku Klux Klan. The group was dedicated to what would come to be defined as "the lost cause," a postwar belief that the Confederacy's purpose was heroic and just. They began menacing black Americans and their Republican allies locally in an effort to retain white supremacy. Later that same year, looking to raise the stakes of the Klan from a local club membership to a nationally recognized organization of influence, they elected their friend Nathan Bedford Forrest, a Democratic National delegate, to the senior position of KKK Grand Wizard. Author

Jack Hurst said of Forrest, "As the Klan's first national leader, he became the Lost Cause's avenging angel, galvanizing a loose collection of boyish secret social clubs into a reactionary instrument of terror still feared today." Under Forrest's leadership, the Klan began a proper reign of terror that consisted of midnight parades, whippings, and murders. By 1868, less than two years after their inauguration, the Ku Klux Klan had infiltrated the Democrat Party's campaign for the presidential reelection. Their efforts began in the spring, with Forrest taking meetings with racist whites throughout Atlanta to organize statewide Klan membership in Georgia. Shortly thereafter, Klansmen strategically murdered George Ashburn, a white man and Republican organizer. Forrest's friend Frank Blair Jr. was nominated as the Democrat vice-presidential candidate, to support New York governor Horatio Seymour, whom they selected to be their presidential hopeful. Their campaign slogan was "Our Ticket, Our Motto, This Is a White Man's Country; Let White Men Rule." But despite their best efforts, Republican presidential nominee Ulysses S. Grant defeated Seymour and won the national election. That is not to say the Klan's efforts were not somewhat successful. In fact, in the states where they murdered the most blacks, Georgia and Louisiana, Grant lost. Today, Democrats will make the claim that the Klan, although led by a Democrat delegate with the express purpose of winning them the upcoming election, was not, technically, established by their party. This is utter nonsense, born of nuance and double-speak. The Klan was created to do their bidding, and led by their party leaders in their effort to do so.

Fortunately, through rigorous policy and reforms, President Grant fundamentally annihilated the Klan, but some forty years later, they would experience what came to be known as their rebirth.

In 1915, white men draped in bedsheets walked down Peachtree Street in Atlanta, firing their rifles in the air to celebrate the release of the silent film *Birth of a Nation*. The feature-length production told the story of the brave sacrifices that the Confederate Klansmen had made to protect the South. The film was an adaptation of the book *The Clansman*, which romanticized and glorified the days of the Ku Klux Klan. The book was written by a man named Thomas Dixon Jr., a dear friend and classmate of incumbent Democrat president Woodrow Wilson. Wilson, himself a racist who began resegregating the federal workforce while in office, made the extraordinary decision to screen the film in the White House. With his patronage, the film became a blockbuster success. It made no difference that the film distorted blacks as rapist villains and whites as their oppressed victims; merchandisers began selling Klan hats and robes. The Klansmen had made a comeback, and it would take many decades before they would lose power again.

It was this "rebirthed" Klan that my grandfather was made to contend with in his youth. What is remarkable, though, is the manner in which my grandfather recounts his dealings with them. My grandfather tells me that Klansmen did not like my great-grandfather. At night, the riders would visit their home and spray bullets through the window. My grandfather says the children would run to the back of home and hide under the bed. "And my daddy would grab the shotgun and shoot back at them boys," he recalls. Though it would be wrong to state that he looks back upon these moments fondly, it is correct to say that he reflects upon them with pride. Not with bitterness, or anger, but pride. I regard his referring to the Klansmen as "boys" as a Freudian slip and a powerful degradation of their desired legacy. My grandfather's memory renders them powerless against his father's fearlessness. Is it not peculiar that those who lived through such evil can speak of those times from a position of such strength, while those who lived not a day of it choose to bemoan it with such cowardice?

I often make the statement that liberalism is a symptom of remarkable privilege. In times of true injustice, no one debates gender pronouns and microaggressions. In times of real conflict, no one demands the government come take their guns. This was especially true for black Americans in the segregated South, during a time when engaging in any inappropriate behavior—hanging out in the streets past dark, public intoxication, using a facility not designated for your skin color—could amount to more than just embarrassment. It could amount to death. Conservatism then is about sense and survival. Leftism is the plaything of a society with too much time on its hands.

My grandfather was sixteen years old when he took a trip up north to Connecticut. He met my grandmother, then phoned his father to say that he wouldn't be coming back home. They married at seventeen years of age. Then, almost four decades later and after raising three children of their own, my three siblings and I moved into their home.

Living with my grandparents was a bit of a culture shock. There were Bible studies every week, prayers before every meal, and more rules than I felt were necessary. Everything centered on the concept of respect and how even our smallest actions were manifestations of character. My grandfather awoke every morning at 4:00 a.m. to fix us a massive southern breakfast ahead of school. We had grits, eggs, bacon, and biscuits, and on special mornings, pancakes, too. Sometimes, in an early morning fog, I or one of my siblings would come down the stairs and silently sit at the dining table. Soon after, we'd discover that our grandfather had prepared a plate for everyone but us. If we'd openly inquire as to the slight, my grandfather would pretend he did not see or hear us. Only then would we remember our offense: we had not greeted him with "good morning." As soon as we'd correct our mistake, my grandfather would look at us warmly, as though we'd just arrived into the room. "Well, hello, baby, how'd you sleep?" he'd say. His point was clear: it was disrespectful not to greet one another. Just one of his many rules.

My grandfather expected my father and older brother to help out with the yard work. My sisters and I, however, were never required to do any such thing. Yard work was a man's job. It was that simple. Instead, my sisters and I, all but a year a part, needed to focus on behaving like respectable young girls. My grandfather would hold doors for us, pull out chairs for us, put our jackets on for us ahead of Sunday service. They say youth is wasted on the young. How I wish I could go back and relish in how positively spoiled I was by my grandparents.

That is not to say that we weren't reprimanded. Our admonishments just came in a different form—and in my young mind, it was the worst form imaginable. There is one instance in particular that has stayed with me always, mainly because it's the only time my grandfather made me cry. One night, I woke up a bit cold. In a slumber, I walked to the thermostat and cranked the heat as far up as it would go. When we awoke, the house was boiling. At breakfast that morning, my grandfather blessed the food and made a particular departure from his usual words. "Dear heavenly father," he began as he always did, "thank you for this food in which we are about to receive." He then unexpectedly interjected, "Lord, please help Candace to realize she should not be messing with the heat in the middle of night . . ." At ten years old, I was positively convinced that my grandfather had a direct line with God almighty Himself. I sprang up from my seat before he could finish, sprinted to my bedroom, and burst into tears. I was embarrassed that my grandfather had discovered my infraction and positively mortified that he had taken the very drastic measure to report it to God. Could it not have been resolved within the lower-level court of family? Was it necessary for him to make an appeal to the supreme court of God? I was inconsolable. Later my grandfather apologized for upsetting me.

Still, his point was clear: there was a hierarchy of authority in the household. And the biblical scripture of Genesis, "what is done in the dark, shall come to light," had never rung more clear.

At around the time that I entered high school, my parents moved us to another side of town. I wish I could say that I remained on the early path that my grandparents had laid before me, but like so many other young Americans, I was lured by a more "liberal" life. I wanted to be cool and liked and normal, so I slipped into a more secular existence that, with time, corroded my values. With my grandparents' watchful gaze no longer a concern, I was free to live as I pleased. There were no more prayers, no more Bible verses, and in just a little time, I came to view my grandparents' teachings as illustrations of my prior bondage.

## A SEASON OF DROUGHT

Much has been whispered about the hate crime that I experienced in high school. Leftists use it as a "gotcha" point. Their less than extraordinary claim is that I "sued my school for racism," thereby proving that racism is real and I am only pretending that it isn't, for profit. My favorite part of this narrative is that it's always presented as an exposé—*we discovered something that Candace Owens doesn't want you to know!*

I laugh at the assertions. Foremost because even a most preliminary of online searches of me will reveal that long before I entered politics, I gave a TEDx talk titled "The Truth About Your Activism," which was about the hate crime that I experienced. So much for trying to hide it! Ironically, it was exactly this experience from my childhood that sobered me to the reality of race, politics, and those who profit from the perpetuation of both.

The story begins one night in 2007, when I was curled up on a couch, watching a film, at my boyfriend's home. Throughout the film, my cell phone kept ringing. Since my service was spotty, I chose to ignore the calls, and set my phone's ringer to silent. In retrospect, it's amazing to consider how that one innocuous decision would transform my life.

Later, when I returned home and my reception was restored, I noticed that there were four voice mails to match the missed calls. I thought it strange that the calls came through back-to-back, and that the anonymous caller decided to leave a message each time. Suddenly worried that there might have been an emergency, I listened to the voice mails:

*Dirty N\*gger . . . We're gonna tar and feather your family. I'm gonna kill you, you know? Just because you're f\*cking poor. And you're black. Okay? You better not be f\*\*cking there, 'cus you might get a bullet in the back on your head. You big whore. You fucking whore . . . Martin Luther King had a dream. Look at that n\*gger, he's dead. That n\*gger is dead! Harriet Tubman—that n\*gger? She's dead, too! Rosa Parks, that f\*cking n\*gger, she's dead!*

They went on and on.

It is difficult to land upon the correct adjectives to convey exactly what I felt when the messages had concluded, except to say that my reaction was physical. It was like having the wind knocked out of my chest—an unexpected force stealing my oxygen immediately. I was overwhelmed and suffocating all at once. The funny thing is that I can still feel it. When I think back to that moment in 2007, I recall every detail so vividly that it makes my heart ache. I ache for high school Candace, alone and crying, unaware of what the next morning would bring. High school Candace couldn't possibly have known it, but the ugliness and hurt would be but a rough pathway to enlightenment.

But there is no portal to our pasts, only our careful retrospective observations, and what will always stun me about that night is the fact that I did nothing and told no one. I was immediately stunned into inaction. I felt fearful, shocked, embarrassed—and remarkably alone.

Call it an opinion, but I believe high school must rank chief among the most traumatizing years of any person's life. It's an awful period of teenage angst and uncertainty, compounded within a threatening timeline of life decisions to be made. Most students are trying to figure out where to fit in socially: what clothes to wear, whose lunch table to sit at, whether or not he/she likes you back. If I had within my possession a time machine that could bring me back to high school, I would set fire to the machine. Truly. The only thing that got me through those years was ego. I wore mine every day like an armor to mask every plausible point of vulnerability. The morning after I received the messages, I felt as though I was dying on the inside, but through the lens of teenage vanity, the inside isn't what counts. And on the outside, I was my usual faux-confident self. I exhibited no signs that I had cried through the night. My first-period class was "Senior Seminar." It was a philosophy course where my teacher encouraged open discussion and debate about politics, current events, and the fallacies that lay between. The style of the class was open forum. I think for many of us, the course became a form of necessary therapy—a rescue from the mounting external pressures that threatened to combust us all. I don't recall what the topic of the day was or what prompted me to raise my hand and volunteer a response to it—but volunteer I did. I can't tell you what response I was looking for in that moment and from that classroom filled with pupils, but I shared it all. Maybe I was just feeling bad for myself. Maybe I wanted to shock them in the way that I had been shocked. Maybe I was looking for sympathy or some general consensus that the world was irrevocably broken, but I made the decision to share it all. And the chain of events that it set off was something that I could have never predicted. In a responsive moment of absolute authority, my teacher commanded me to "get up" and follow him to the principal's office. Upon hearing the voicemail messages, she immediately phoned the police. And my entire life transformed thereafter.

It would turn out that the perpetrators were a group of boys led by my former friend Zack. Zack was upset that I had started a relationship with my boyfriend and had less time for him, so when he and his three friends (whom I had never so much as met) found themselves bored and under the influence one night, prank-calling me seemed to be a perfectly reasonable way to pass the time. Incidentally, one of Zack's friends happened to be the fourteen-year-old son of our city's mayor (and the future Democrat governor of Connecticut), Dannel Malloy.

For the media, the political connection proved irresistible.

Within days, my face was splattered across the front page of every newspaper across the state, and I was a repeat story on the evening news. They played the voice mails ad nauseam. Since none of the boys would formally admit to their role, and because a politician's son was involved, the police brought in the FBI to help analyze the voice mails.

My town was divided by the sensationalism. It felt as though every single person, teacher, student, and parent alike had entered in a social verdict. There were some people who were convinced I was lying. Since Zack was adamantly and boldly declaring to our classmates that he took no part in it, some began to invest in the Machiavellian narrative that I had phoned myself. More innocently, others believed that I was simply accusing the wrong guy.

As the leading bastion of progressivism and civil rights, the NAACP were more than happy to insert themselves into the narrative. They beelined to the front steps of my high school, where they greeted news cameras anxious to receive statements pertaining to the injustices of the investigation.

To their credit, they rightfully called out the unusual delay of justice that was more than likely tied to the case's political angle. Administrators from my school were protecting the perpetrators because of the mayor's son, and the NAACP took them to task. What the NAACP did not do, however, was ever actually speak to me. I never had an interview or a meeting with any of my so-called allies who were so eager to speak out about racism but not interested in me, the real person at the center of the story.

It took six weeks before the FBI investigation concluded, before the articles stopped being written, before the opinion letters to the editors stopped accompanying every newspaper, and before my name was officially cleared as a co-conspirator in my own case. As it turned out, I had *not* phoned myself. Subsequently, arrests were made and charges were brought. I was labeled, officially, as the victim. And then everybody disappeared. Everybody but me, of course. I was left to deal with the emotional roller coaster of sudden, unwanted infamy and controversy, followed by utter desertion.

If this narrative sounds familiar to you, it may be because it has become part and parcel of our mainstream media agenda. A school shooting takes place, only to have the survivors hijacked by gun control activists looking to jam through their policies in a time of high emotion. A black man is killed by a police officer, and his image is used to further the narrative that white cops are murdering black men for sport.

Over and over again, somebody else's real pain and tragedy are reduced to media talking points to further a political agenda. Emotions are elicited and concern is feigned until a bigger story comes around.

This soured my perspective on the world early in life. Fundamentally, I began to believe that the world was happening to me, that I was a tragic Shakespearean figure doomed to fail because of the unfortunate circumstances of my childhood. This quite naturally led me down a path of liberating myself from any concept of personal responsibility. I drank, I partied, I got into fights. Everywhere in my life I created chaos because chaos came to falsely represent a state of freedom. I felt freed from rules, freed from regulations, freed from any accountability. And because I felt that my life's narrative had been decided for me, I turned to anorexia to reassert control. For four years, I restricted how many calories I consumed. The lighter I felt I could make myself physically, the lighter I felt mentally. I felt freed from the weight of my past.

But with time, what was supposed to feel like freedom began to feel like bondage. I was pretending that a life with no rules made me feel freer, when in reality it made me feel insecure. I was losing more than pounds. I was losing myself.

This was leftism unleashed.

## HARVESTING CONSERVATIVE SEEDS

There is a Bible proverb that reads "Train up a child in the way he should go, And when he is old, he will not depart from it."

In early 2013, I got a call that my grandmother was sick. By this time, my grandparents had moved back to Fayetteville, North Carolina. In their retirement they purchased property and built their dream home upon a plot of land that my grandfather knew well; it was the sharecropping farm that he grew up on.

We were told that my grandmother would be out of the hospital by the end of the week. I packed a bag and traveled from New York to Fayetteville to visit her anyway—and I wasn't the only one. As a symbol of her matriarchy, everyone got on a plane: cousins, brothers, sisters, and aunts. For the woman who had given us her all, we knew we needed to show up. The doctors insisted that she would be released in two days. As it turned out, she would be dead in two weeks.

Unaware that it was the last time I would see her, I spent most of my time bragging to her about my fancy new job in New York City. In retrospect, I think my grandmother knew somehow—she knew the doctors had missed something and that she would never return home. She took care to speak to each of us in such a way that she hadn't before.

When my grandmother turned her attention to me, I exuded my practiced confidence. I showed her an expensive new designer bag I had just purchased and told her all about my new job in private equity. I thought she would be proud of me, proud of how successful I was becoming. I thought wrong.

My grandmother, as she always did, saw right through the facade. "Candace," she began, "I worry about you in New York. I feel like you are losing yourself." I told her I was fine and not to worry. Believing that she would indeed be discharged in forty-eight hours, I bid her farewell and told her I would call her in a few days. That was the last conversation I ever had with her. She died ten days later, a shock and blow to my family that is still felt today.

Grief consumed me. Guilt consumed me. And while the grief was foreign, I knew the guilt well. Because there had been a quiet voice that had been with me since that high school hate crime, one that I chose to muffle, over and over again, from the back of my mind. That voice, gentle as it were, was unrelenting. It was patient, it was kind, but it was unrelenting, and the question was always the same:

*Are you yet ready to set down the weight of victimhood? Are you ready to run this race of life, truly free?*

And suddenly I was ready. I was ready to become how my grandparents had raised me. I replayed my grand-mother's last words in my head. She was right, I was losing myself. I recognized that my current worldview was not serving me. I needed to change my perspective, and I started by asking myself a simple question:

*What if the world is not happening to Candace Owens? What if Candace Owens is happening to the world?*

It was a daunting question. It implied that nothing was owed to me and that even those situations that were not necessarily my fault were, in the end, certainly going to be my problems to contend with. I embarked on a personal audit of my life that brought me to a deeper consideration of my grandparents' sacrifices. While my grandfather was growing up on a sharecropping farm, drying tobacco, my grandmother was living in the Virgin Islands, unwanted be-cause she was considered crippled. At just ten years old, she spent a full year of her life hospitalized after a surgery to correct her hips. I had never known my grandmother to walk without a limp. She lived in a constant state of physical pain. But never once had she or my grandfather ever complained. They did not complain as children, nor did they complain as adults, not even as they were forced to contend with the world's problems in addition to their own. Yet there I was, with a full-fledged victim mentality, upset that life hadn't been *fair* to me. It was pathetic.

I knew it was time. It was time to return to the only values and principles that had ever made me feel truly content.

The first principle was to refuse the victim narrative. If my grandfather could reduce the Klansmen to "boys," surely I was capable of reassessing my own points of victimhood.

And so I mentally revisited the high school hate crime. In retrospect, I found it interesting to consider that in today's society, we have developed something of an obsession with determining a victim and a villain, and then closing the door on any further analysis. Maybe we ought to blame Disney movies—our earliest point of indoctrination that there needs to be a hero and a bad guy in every story line. The hero wins, the villain loses, and the credits role. Off-screen, journalists have taken on the responsibility of passing judgment within the confines of absolute goodness or badness. Such blanket assessments have proven to be a profitable model, because sensationalism and hyperbole sell. Of course, humanity is much more complex than we'd like to believe. If the media had any nerve to dig beyond "racist white boys" phone "victim black girl," they may have accidentally landed upon a much more human narrative.

As I mentioned earlier, Zack (who was dubbed by the media as the "ringleader" of the attack) was my former friend. That fact alone, under even amateur analysis, should have served as a clue that his actions were not inspired by deeply held racist views. Prior to the voice mails, Zack and I had spent nearly every day together over the course of a school year doing what high schoolers do: eating junk food, talking about dreams, unloading our anxieties. Then rather abruptly, I got a boyfriend and all of that ended. I became every bit the stereotype of a young teenage girl in love; I stopped hanging out with my friends, and my every second became about my new relationship.

If all of this sounds remarkably immature, it's because it was. It was textbook, meaningless high school drama that led to a series of irreversible events. It is likely that after losing someone whom he trusted and confided in daily, Zack was hurt. It is likely that under the influence of alcohol, that hurt morphed into anger and in a moment of childish impulse and stupidity, he thought, "What can I say to make Candace hurt in the way that I am in hurting?" It is likely that in thinking of the most hurtful and hateful things he could possibly say to make me hurt, he chose racial slurs. People don't like to hear that assessment because it's too human. It doesn't feed the media beast. It doesn't quench our insatiable thirst to quickly identify evil and socially cancel the evildoer. I sometimes wonder if we so often seek to point out ugliness as a cheap formulaic way to convince ourselves that we are good.

*Look what that bad person did. I would never do that. Therefore, I am good.*

The resulting truth is that the media's surface analysis of that night destroyed five lives: the four young boys, who were publicly stained as racists before they began their lives, and me, who was publicly labeled a victim before I had begun mine.

I knew what Zack did that night was wrong, and I had no doubt that his actions deserved consequence. But now, in a return to my conservative principles, I was wondering whether there was any permanence to his wrongful action, or to my victimhood. Could I evolve? Could he evolve? And who are those who insist that we ought not to?

## RETURNING TO OUR CONSERVATIVE ROOTS

The glorification of victimhood is exclusively promoted by the Left. It becomes necessary that I first define exactly what I mean when I refer to "leftists" and "liberals" throughout this book and why I will, at many times, use their identities interchangeably.

Liberalism is defined as a political philosophy based on liberty and equality before the law. It is an allegiance to a set of principles that guarantee those who follow them, a society with more individual freedoms. True liberalism pursues principles like the right to life, right to vote, freedom of speech, etc. (When our forefathers wrote "Right to life," liberty, and the pursuit of happiness they meant a right to life—literally). On behalf of black America, I will make an argument that liberalism has only ever been practiced by conservatives in this country.

Leftism is defined as any political philosophy that seeks to infringe upon individual liberties in its demand for a higher moral good. Leftists concern themselves not with principle, but with some greater morality that must be achieved. The issue with leftism is that moral goodness is, of course, subjective. Not so long ago, white supremacy was deemed the higher moral good, and in its pursuit, leftists infringed upon the rights of black Americans. Today, economic equality is the established higher moral good the Left is after, and we will soon unpack just how many liberties have been arrested in its pursuit.

So why are we seeing resurgent conservatism throughout Western societies? Because self-described "liberals," those who like to view themselves as centrists are realizing that the hallowed middle ground of politics has been consumed by leftism. Leftists have been able to operate under the guise of liberalism, by claiming to want a certain *type* of equality. But demanding economic equality can be accomplished only by infringing upon individual liberties. The nuance here is important. Both liberals and leftists find themselves allied by the concept of equality, and an inability to recognize that their goals stand in radical opposition to one another. In essence, there is nothing more illiberal than leftism. And although many liberals have awoken themselves to this impossible partnership, others remain unable to achieve such clarity.

Alas, what remains of the doomed union between liberals and leftists exists under the Democrat Party, a political group that champions leftist solutions to the perpetual detriment of black America. The entire Democrat platform is built upon an everlasting stream of victims versus oppressors, and black America is their favored horse to bet on when it comes to jamming through their policies.

In the Left's oversimplified version of American history, blacks are a permanent underclass who must commit their votes to Democrat politicians for rescuing. Democrats see inherent racism and struggle in nearly everything, thereby destroying nearly all racial progress that has been achieved thus far.

The sad truth is that nearly every policy they promote invariably *harms* black America. Indeed, there is something about progressive policies that always leads to regressive results for black America.

But what if black America simply refused their offers? What if we formally rejected the victim narrative, thereby rejecting the slow poison of leftist policies? What might happen if black America collectively called the Left's bluff on racism—thereby reducing their claims of perpetual victimhood to the ill-effective emotional strategy that it is? Could we, collectively, make a return to our conservative roots?

# 2

## ON FAMILY

The last few years have brought an unforeseen spread of conservatism in the West. The 2016 vote for "BREXIT"—the British exit from the European union—shocked every mainstream pundit and poll worldwide that had bet against it. After forty-three years of the United Kingdom's forfeiting its sovereignty to bureaucrats in Brussels, British citizens had had enough. Despite being warned that their departure might lead to their economic demise, the United Kingdom voted to leave.

Similarly, on the other side of the Atlantic, Donald Trump's defeat of presidential hopeful Hillary Clinton—

a Washington insider who was glorified by the press—sent shock waves throughout the world. For the mainstream media characters who had grown used to reporting what *should* happen, rather than what actually *could* happen, these binary political earthquakes could mean only one thing: widespread disobedience. Voters had *disobeyed* the mainstream narrative. In response, left-wing journalists, unused to having their authority questioned, began printing articles claiming that people were becoming "radicalized by the internet." This, of course, is a laugh-out-loud assertion born of journalists' anxiety that they are ceding influence to independent voices.

And indeed they are.

On any given day, CNN, the largest left-wing cable news station in America, averages 706,000 viewers. When the world depended upon television as its primary source of information, that may have been considered a large reach, but technology has transformed our circumstances. Today, the world prefers to communicate online, and so although leftists dominate the TV market, conservatives are winning the internet.

As an example, according to Twitter analytics, just one solitary tweet that I send reaches an average of 2.5 million people. This means that I am able to dwarf all of CNN's viewership with a tweet—and I'm far from the only person with that capability.

Realizing that none of their ideas were being presented across the mainstream networks, conservatives began mining the Wild West of the early social media age and found success. Social media, then, represents an existential threat to the left-wing establishment, which is why they have begun pressuring social media companies to both ban and limit the reach of conservative accounts. This explains why, in a 2018 opinion piece, the *New York Times* issued the rather extraordinary claim that "jihadists and right-wing extremists use remarkably similar social media strategies." In December of that same year, the *Daily Beast* published an article titled "How YouTube Built a Radicalization Machine for the Right." Thousands upon thousands of articles were written conveying the same sentiment: the internet was suddenly a problem. Of course, what was really happening was that the Left's majority coverage (Democrat journalists outnumber Republicans 4 to 1) was now made to compete with the Right in getting out information. With a swell of independent voices rising, they were simply ill prepared to have their narratives challenged.

Unsurprisingly, there were no feverish claims of internet radicalization until America voted for Donald Trump. Despite the mainstream media's spending every hour portraying him as a racist, sexist monster, when it came time, America ignored their smears and picked him to lead the nation. The journalists were correct to blame our collective disobedience on the internet. We disobeyed because we were able to determine, independently, that the media was attempting to skew the election against him, and they were using extravagant claims of "racism" to do it.

I was one such person who was "radicalized" on the internet during this time, meaning that I too learned the truth about the media's distortions and lies. Armed with nothing more than a hunch that the media's insistence on racial unrest was suspicious, I turned to the internet to investigate some varied opinions on the mainstream's position that a Donald Trump presidency would inspire a white supremacist uprising.

## MY "RADICALIZATION"

When I first became curious about conservative perspectives, I began searching YouTube for "black conservatives," people I had previously dismissed as "Uncle Toms" and "race-traitors." At the time of my searching, there was an ongoing mainstream narrative about the topic of police brutality. I decided to start there.

I came across a clip of Larry Elder, a black radio show host, author, former attorney, and self-professed libertarian. Elder has dedicated decades to exposing the hypocrisies of the Left. With books like *What's Race Got to Do With It?*, he has developed expert analyses on the issues crippling black Americans today.

In the now-viral clip, Elder sits across from liberal host Dave Rubin (now a dear friend of mine) for an interview on his Web show, *The Rubin Report*. With the amiable intent of acknowledging systemic issues of oppression facing black America, Rubin makes the fatal mistake of suggesting that police brutality is a blatant example of racism. And with sharpshooting statistical accuracy, Elder responds with a total annihilation of the liberal narrative:

"Nine hundred sixty-five people were shot by cops last year. Four percent of them were white cops shooting unarmed blacks. In Chicago in 2011, twenty-one people were shot and killed by cops. In 2015 there were seven. In Chicago (which is about one-third black, one-third white, and one-third Hispanic) 70 percent of homicides are black on black—about forty per month, almost five hundred last year in Chicago—and about 75 percent of them are unsolved. Where's the Black Lives Matter on that? The idea that a racist white cop shooting unarmed black people is a peril to black people is complete and total B.S."

I knew that I had just witnessed an intellectual beat-down and that Dave Rubin wasn't the only victim. In the span of fifteen seconds, Elder had knocked me into the reality that many of the issues I had accepted to be meaningful on the basis of excessive media coverage were of very little substance. With humility, Rubin then asked Larry what *his* opinion was on issues facing black America.

"The biggest burden that black people have in my opinion is the percentage of blacks 75 percent of them—that are raised without fathers. And that has every other social negative consequence connected to it: crime, not being able to compete economically in the country, being more likely to be arrested, that's the number one problem facing the black community."

Rubin, quickly beginning to see the light, asked Elder what could be done to tackle that problem, to which Elder boldly declared, "Reverse the welfare state. In 1890–1900, you look at the sentence reports, a black person—believe it or not—was slightly more likely to be born to a nuclear intact family than a white kid. Even during slavery a black kid was more likely to be born under a roof with his biological mother and biological father than today."

Larry's declaration that even during the traumatic periods of slavery and segregation, black families were more intact than they are today, stunned me. I wanted to learn more.

The destruction of the family unit used to be considered a moral abomination, so much so that it became the cornerstone of the abolitionist movement. Harriet Beecher Stowe's *Uncle Tom's Cabin*, widely regarded as one of the most effective tools in shifting the attitudes of northern whites against slavery, is a 250-plus-page lament on slavery's effects on the black family. *Uncle Tom's Cabin* is a chilling illustration of a father who learns that he will be sold away from his wife and children and a mother who discovers that she will be separated from her only living child. The cultural impact of the book cannot be overstated; families gathered together after dinner to read the controversial tome that pulled back the veil on the country's most heinous institution. Readers in the northern United States, as well as in Europe, became outraged by—and sympathetic to—the atrocities detailed by Stowe.

Of course, the formal ending of the practice of slavery became monumental in the legitimizing of black families across America. Tera Hunter, a history professor at Princeton University, spoke about this revolution in a 2010 interview with NPR. "After the Civil War, you see marriage being one of the first civil rights that African Americans are able to exercise," she explained. "And they do that with a great deal of enthusiasm, to the point of overwhelming the Union Army, making it difficult for them to handle the numbers of people trying to get married." Additionally, millions of former slaves conducted desperate, long-distance searches to reconnect with family members who had been sold away or otherwise displaced by the war. The result was the formation and committed maintenance of millions of black families. In many regards, the preservation of the family became greater than the preservation of self, a sentiment shared by men and women of all races throughout history.

How is it possible, then, that some one hundred years *after* slavery, the great rupture of the black family began? If not even slavery or Jim Crow laws could break down the black family, if not even the inhumanity of being deemed three-fifths of a person, or being granted just a fraction of the rights of others was capable of tearing them apart—what ultimately did?

## LBJ's GREAT FAILURE

The Democrat Party has a long history of racism, but few can claim as much credit for damaging the black community as the late president Lyndon B. Johnson. Robert Caro's definitive biography of LBJ, *Master of the Senate*, talks about his common use of the word "nigger," not in singular use, but frequently and repeatedly. While in Congress, Johnson was an extremely conscientious member of the Southern Bloc, the Democrat-controlled voting group that was notoriously committed to blocking the progression of civil rights. In fact, during Johnson's first twenty years in the U.S. Senate, he voted down every single civil rights measure that made the floor.

Despite this track record, Johnson is hailed as a hero because it was his presidential inking of the Civil Rights Act of 1964 that granted black Americans equal standing in the eyes of the law with whites. But just how does Johnson's signature on this act of freedom reconcile with his earlier voting record, use of racist terminology, as well as his well-documented discriminatory treatment of blacks around him? After decades of working against blacks, had Johnson experienced a sudden epiphany?

There is a quote that is attributed to LBJ in Ronald

Kessler's book *Inside the White House* that may be spurious (we shall never know as it was not verbally recorded), where LBJ allegedly said to two governors, "I'll have those niggers voting Democrat for the next two hundred years." His reference, according to Kessler, was not to the Civil Rights Act of 1964, nor to the Voting Rights Act of 1965, but instead to the launch of the Great Society program— the method by which the Democrat Party would marry black America to the government, via welfare.

LBJ's Great Society initiatives were a deliberate attack on the black family unit, levied through the empowerment of the poor black woman and the emasculation—and ultimate obviation—of the black man. Johnson's promise to eradicate poverty in all of America was fully embraced by struggling blacks, so much so that they did not object to rules that rendered poor mothers ineligible for benefits when an able-bodied male was present. Black women were instead encouraged, by their government, to raise children alone.

Emboldened by the appeal of free government money, many of the pro-family advancements made by a post-slavery black community were quickly rolled back. As some black women discovered that the government could act as provider for their families, they often neglected to hold black men accountable to their children, which over time can lead to choosing less suitable partners for marriage and fatherhood. Government assistance also provides no incentive to black men to step up. This was the first major indentation that the government made upon black culture. Today, hearing black hip-hop artists rap and sing about their various "baby-mamas" is considered culturally normative.

There is a lot of data freely available on the decline of black America between the initiation of the Great Society and the current day, but one statistic is startling. According to the *Statistical Abstract of the United States*, in 1963, 72 percent of nonwhite families were married and together. By 2017 that data was almost exactly reversed: only 27 percent of black households were married, a staggering 45 percent drop over the period. In comparison, the white population went from 89 percent married and together in 1963, down to 51 percent in 2017, a 38 percent comparative drop. Policies that were purported to "empower" black America actually resulted in the greatest family breakdown across all demographics. Another telling area of breakdown is the number of unmarried men there are in the black community. In the 1960 census, approximately 24.4 percent of white men were unmarried aged fifteen and over; the comparable data point within the black community was 29.6 percent, an approximate 5 percent difference. Compare this with current rates of unmarried men today: in 2017, 33.1 percent of white men were unmarried, while unmarried black men had risen to a staggering 51.9 percent, a variation of 18.8 percent—or, in other words, a variation jump of 362 percent.

It is a correct assumption that these single men are not all committing themselves to lives of virtuous chastity. The majority go through what is now a normalized pattern of unmarried sexual relationships, with a high probability of fatherhood. Exceptional rates of father absence can go a long way in terms of explaining racial disparities. What the Great Society programs proved was that in the absence of fathers, children will pursue that missing paternity elsewhere, and elsewhere tends to be the streets, where an easy path to crime, and eventually prison, awaits.

Larry Elder was correct then to point to father absence as the greatest index of predictive failure. According to the independent, nonpartisan Brookings Institution:

*Children raised by single mothers are more likely to fare worse on a number of dimensions, including their*

*school achievement, their social and emotional develop-*
*ment, their health, and their success in the labor mar-*
*ket. They are at great risk of parental abuse and neglect*
*(especially from live-in boyfriends who are not their bi-*
*ological fathers), more likely to become teen parents and*
*less likely to graduate from high school or college.*

What is more, the tendency of black children raised in fatherless homes to perpetuate the environments into which they were born puts continued pressure on the government to support future generations of fatherless offspring.

In the generations since the implementation of Johnson's Great Society, the epidemic of fatherless homes has produced a modernized, black family dynamic that functions nothing like the model sought by early-twentieth-century blacks. The results have been exactly as dramatic as Johnson and his Democrat cronies could have dreamed. When we consider where black America is today versus before the initiation of the Great Society reforms, it's suddenly much easier to reconcile LBJ's racism. What better way to connive an entire ethnic group into believing that you are for them than through the enactment of pieces of legislation that will guarantee their votes for the next "two hundred years"? LBJ, arguably one of the greatest "politicians" of twentieth-century America, both convinced black America that he was their greatest savior and ensured that they would forever be in need of saving. Black America was both freed and enslaved again within one presidency.

In effect, the policies that were purported to "empower" black America and bridge the wealth divide between whites and blacks have only exacerbated that divide, with the added benefit of placing a tremendous strain on our national Treasury.

Welfare is the largest expenditure in the federal budget—more than $1 trillion, yearly—with absolutely no empirical points of success that warrant its continued existence. "What if I took that kind of 'welfare' policy and implemented it in your family?" wrote Kay Coles James, president of the Heritage Foundation. "If I said to your sons, 'Sweetie, you don't have to work; I'll take care of everything,' and if I said to your daughters, 'Sugar, you go ahead and have as many babies as you want; I'll give you more money to take care of them,' what do you think your family would be like in 20 years? I'll tell you: Your sons would be living at home and not working, your daughters would be having kids out of wedlock, and your family would be a whole lot poorer."

It surprises me that the issue of welfare reform has been drawn across party lines, when politicians on both sides of the aisle have justifiably critiqued the modern social safety net and its tendency to keep blacks tight within its perimeters. Ronald Reagan was roundly lambasted for his depiction of the "welfare queen"—a woman who was said to have used "80 names, 30 addresses, 15 telephone numbers to collect food stamps, Social Security, veterans' benefits for four nonexistent deceased veteran husbands," and a woman whose "tax-free cash income alone has been running $150,000 a year," and who, for better or worse, was said to represent the vast majority of urban (read: black) women on welfare. Despite criticism, Reagan was telling the truth. Welfarism wreaks undue havoc upon any given society by enabling irresponsible behavior from both men and women.

Those who wish to dismiss that truth as the racist rantings of a now-deceased, staunchly conservative Republican president would do well to remember that its sentiments were also echoed by former president Barack Obama, our liberal, first black president.

In an impassioned 2008 Father's Day speech, Obama made clear the impact that single-parent homes—a direct result of the welfare state—were having upon black children. He said:

> *Of all the rocks upon which we build our lives, we are reminded today that family is the most important. And we*

*are called to recognize and honor how critical every fa-
ther is to that foundation. They are teachers and coaches.
They are mentors and role models. They are examples of
success and the men who constantly push us toward it.*

*But if we are honest with ourselves, we'll admit that
what too many fathers also are is missing—missing from
too many lives and too many homes. They have abandoned
their responsibilities, acting like boys instead of men. And
the foundations of our families are weaker because of it.*

---

Obama continued:

*You and I know how true this is in the African-
American community. We know that more than half
of all black children live in single-parent households,
a number that has doubled—doubled—since we were
children. We know the statistics—that children who
grow up without a father are five times more likely
to live in poverty and commit crime, nine times more
likely to drop out of schools, and twenty times more
likely to end up in prison. They are more likely to have
behavioral problems or run away from home or become*

*teenage parents themselves. And the foundations of our
community are weaker because of it.*

In the twelve years since Obama delivered that moving
speech, our society seems to have barreled further away
from its lessons. The general shifting of American culture
toward liberal ideologies has loosened the stigma of out-of-
wedlock childbirth among all races. We are engaged in a
cultural war—one that is being waged between those who
uphold the traditional values responsible for our country's
achievements, and those pushing for an updated, faux-
progressive, radically destructive change.

I have often said that no society can survive without
strong men. Radical feminists regularly insinuate that accepting the empirical evidence that children fare better
with their fathers in the home suggests that women ought
to remain in abusive relationships if they become pregnant.
This is a twisted, neoliberal assessment that works to de-
value the presence of men, through the argument of an extreme. Of course, no women (or men, for that matter)
should remain in abusive situations for the sake of children, and of course there are plenty of examples of single
parents raising their children up to be successful adults.

But these represent exceptions, not the rule. As a rule, children fare better in two-parent homes. We should not uphold exceptions as proof that women do not need husbands and children do not need male guidance. If given the choice, we should always seek to provide children with the head start that comes from being raised in a healthy, two-parent environment.

## BLACK GENOCIDE, LIBERAL SUPPORT

In 1965, a man by the name of Daniel Patrick Moynihan made the terrible mistake of telling the truth. As the assistant secretary of labor, he was asked to study black poverty, during the time when America had just formally acknowledged the wrongs of segregation. With this acknowledgment came the fashionable belief that black people could no longer be held responsible for anything. Every ill that had befallen our community from that point onward became viewed as a legacy of white supremacy. In essence, black Americans became blameless. So when Daniel Patrick Moynihan issued his study, *The Negro Family: The Case for National Action*, and highlighted the collapse of black marriages in America as a contributing factor to black poverty, he was roundly condemned for "victim-blaming." It would take decades before experts agreed that everything he had reported was accurate.

Also buried in his report was another data point that was likely to strike fear into the hearts of any racists who were intent on maintaining the status quo. Moynihan noted that the black population was growing. Beginning in the 1950s, the black population grew at a rate of 2.4 percent per year compared to 1.7 percent for the total population, leading Moynihan to write, "[if] this rate continues, in seven years, 1 American in 8 will be nonwhite."

Efforts to control the black population had been in place since at least the 1920s, when fear began spreading around the nation that the preferred, more intelligent white race was becoming threatened by immigration. Popular eugenicists made the argument that it was necessary to make efforts to stop those who were deemed undesirable, from reproducing. Margaret Sanger, the founder of Planned Parenthood—who is today hailed as a hero for giving women greater control over when they bear children—was one such eugenicist. Sanger upheld the popular belief of her day that America needed to hinder those with unfavorable traits from reproducing.

From 1939 to 1942, Sanger led the Negro Project, an initiative that was purported to combat poverty among southern blacks by providing family planning education and access to birth control and contraceptives. Intentional as she was, Sanger pushed to partner with black ministers, who she knew would be instrumental in gaining the trust of the people she was looking to "help" and might thereby conceal her true motives.

Sanger wrote to Dr. Clarence Gamble, another leader of the Negro Project, "The minister's work is also important and also he should be trained, perhaps by the [Birth Control] Federation [of America] as to our ideals and the goal that we hope to reach."

While Sanger's appeal to the black community may have been about "choice," the fact remains that she openly authored articles in support of "applying a stern and rigid policy of sterilization" in an effort to "insure the country against future burdens of maintenance for numerous offspring as may be born of feeble-minded parents." So ingratiated were her ideas with the racism of her time that she addressed Ku Klux Klan members to garner further support for her birth control measures.

At the turn of the twentieth century, the eugenicist sentiment became a growing movement in America. The list of those deemed "unfit" included immigrants, the physically and mentally disabled, the impoverished, the stupid, and of course, blacks. The practice of forced sterilization upon black women in the rural South was so common it became known as Mississippi appendectomies: doctors would tell women that they needed to have their appendixes removed but would instead rob them of their reproductive abilities.

In 1921, Sanger founded the American Birth Control League, which would eventually become the Planned Parenthood Federation of America, today the largest provider of abortions in the United States. And since 1973, when abortions became legal, black women have terminated far more pregnancies than women of any other race. According to 2016 data from the Centers for Disease Control and Prevention, with 401 abortions per 1,000 live births, black women have the highest abortion ratio among racial groups—far higher than the 109 abortions per 1,000 live births of white women. Despite representing just 13 percent of the United States female population, they make up nearly 40 percent of all abortions. What is more, research conducted by the Life Issues Institute found that "79 percent of abortion-offering Planned Parenthood facilities are within walking distance of black or Hispanic neighborhoods," and "62 percent are near black neighborhoods." This data clearly speaks to the intentional targeting of the black community, much in the same way that Margaret Sanger's Negro Project targeted poor black women in the South.

Of course, this ugly truth regarding Sanger's legacy has been pardoned by liberals who continue to carry out her agenda. And with more than 19 million black babies having been aborted since 1973, one black pastor was right to warn that "If the current trend [of abortions in the black community] continues, by 2038 the black vote will be insignificant." According to a Pew research report, the birth rate for blacks declined 29 percent between 1990 and 2010.

It's no wonder Democrats have suddenly come out in support of mass illegal immigration, as a new victim class to carry their party will be needed in the near future. Democrats continue to champion abortion as "reproductive health care." And in the same way that the welfare system works to enable irresponsible behavior, so too does the abortion—industry—except this time, parents can abandon the responsibility of taking care of their children while they're in the womb.

Rev. Dr. Luke Bobo, an anti-abortion pastor from Kansas City, Missouri, told the *New York Times*, "Those who are most vocal about abortion and abortion laws are my white brothers and sisters, and yet many of them do not care about the plight of the poor, the plight of the immigrant, the plight of African Americans. My argument here is let us think about the entire life span of the person."

Thinking about the entire life span of a person is a historically conservative position. It was President Reagan who cleverly remarked on the irony—that every person who is for abortion has already been born. Hypocrisy, though, has come to define the Left's various platforms. Is it not a wonder that the same party that claims that racism is at the core of black American ills routinely promotes the policies and ideologies that victimize black families the most? The same people who scream about black incarceration rates, economic disparities, and impoverished neighborhoods never lend their voices in attacks against the welfare system, which inspires all three. Similarly, is it not a wonder that the same people behind the Black Lives Matter campaign, the ones who claim to care about the unjust slaughter of blacks in the streets, refuse to acknowledge that today the most unsafe place for a black child is in its mother's womb? Indeed, perhaps the reason Democrats don't attack these industries is that they are the authors, perpetrators, and main benefactors of their Machiavellian designs.

3

# ON FEMINISM

There are so many different channels and underground passages through which the Left funnels its poison to black America. The one that I have been the most outspoken against is feminism. What even is feminism? The first answer that seems true is that nobody knows anymore. A movement that was born out of noble and humble beginnings in a search for equality of opportunity between the sexes has now devolved into something quite different and altogether unrecognizable from its initial nascent form. Modern feminism is now the plaything of the Left; it is the harbinger term for a witch hunt against all men. This time, though, the witches are doing the hunting.

In the last three years, since the #MeToo movement has taken hold and caught fire, leftists have done everything in their power to divide the nation into two groups: feminists and antifeminists. In the process, an effort that was launched to call attention to rampant sexual abuse and harassment in the entertainment industry has somehow devolved into a trend of denigrating any person, male or female, who does not blindly support the Left's modern feminist agenda.

I, of course, fall into this group because I am an avowed antifeminist, but does that mean that I support the subjugation or harassment of women? Of course not. Nor do I support the subjugation and harassment of men, which is exactly what modern feminism does.

Nothing about modern feminism, commonly termed "intersectional feminism," has anything to do with its original search for equality. Indeed, the founders of the feminist movement, more commonly termed "first-wave feminism," would see none of their original movement in what the word is used to encompass now. Voting rights for women, equal legal standing with men, a recognition of women as equally capable and competent in most workplaces, and the ending of gender-based discrimination—

these goals have, for all intents and purposes, been achieved. This is not to say that pockets of sexism do not still exist; of course prejudice in all its forms maintains its hideouts in modern society. But the modern feminist movement works only to exacerbate these issues.

The truth is that as a woman in America today, I am now not only on equal footing, but in fact positively discriminated in favor of, by employers over men. As a woman in 2020, I have a greater life expectancy, a greater probability of receiving a college education, and in many professions a greater likelihood of employment with more years to enjoy my pension and a greater array of benefits available to me than a man. This is why I so proudly declare that I am not a feminist. Rather, I feel positively affirmed in my femininity.

## FEMINISM IS DESIGNED TO PROTECT PRIVILEGED LIBERAL WOMEN

It should first be made clear that Democrats do not care if you believe women. They just want you to believe *their* women.

Brett Michael Kavanaugh, appointed to the Court of Appeals for the D.C. Circuit in 2006 under President

George W. Bush, was nominated by President Trump on July 9, 2018, to take the then-vacant position of Justice Anthony Kennedy on the Supreme Court. In his remarks after being nominated, Kavanaugh said, "No president has ever consulted more widely or talked with more people from more backgrounds to seek input about a Supreme Court nomination." Kavanaugh would be drawn from the same D.C. Circuit that has given rise to the appointments of Justices Roberts, Thomas, Ginsburg, and Scalia; his path to the Supreme Court included Yale University, Yale Law School, clerking at the U.S. Court of Appeals for the Third and Ninth Circuits, clerking for Justice Kennedy at the Supreme Court, working for Ken Starr (former solicitor general of the United States), working for the legal team of President George W. Bush, working for the private practice of Kirkland & Ellis as partner, and, of course, serving as a U.S. circuit judge. Yet this impressive track record of legal scholarship and experience was to simply be discarded by the Democrats as they unleashed the true horror of leftist feminism upon him. Christine Blasey Ford, a registered Democrat and financial contributor to leftist political organizations, came forward as his chief accuser before other speculative witnesses also emerged from the woodwork. Ford accused Kavanaugh of having forced himself on her at a house party in the summer of 1982, when he was seventeen and Ford fifteen. Her written testimony before the Senate Judicial Committee accused Kavanaugh of violent attempted rape at that house party in an upstairs bedroom with Mark Judge, a school friend of Kavanaugh's, who she claimed was also present:

*I believed he was going to rape me. I tried to yell for help. When I did, Brett put his hand over my mouth to stop me from screaming. That was what terrified me the most, and has had the most lasting impact on my life. It was hard for me to breathe, and I thought that Brett was accidentally going to kill me.*

Ford named three men and one woman in her testimony: Brett Kavanaugh, Mark Judge, Patrick Smyth, and "my friend Leland Ingham." It must have therefore been difficult for Ford to learn that both Judge and Smyth denied any recollection of having attended such a party. On top of that, her "lifelong friend" Ingham (a phrase used by Ford) released a statement via her attorney that said, "Simply put, Ms. Keyser [nee Ingham] does not know Mr. Kavanaugh, and she has no recollection of ever being at a party or gathering where he was present, with or without Dr. Ford." This must have been especially hard for Ford's lawyer, Debra Katz, to hear, although was it not slightly suspicious that Ford would pick Debra Katz as her attorney? In a *Washington Post* puff piece titled "Christine Blasey Ford's lawyer Debra Katz: The feared attorney of the #MeToo moment," the author Isaac Stanley-Becker writes:

> *By her own words, she [Debra Katz] is part of the resistance to the Trump administration's agenda. "This administration's explicit agenda is to wage an assault on our most basic rights—from reproductive rights to our rights to fair pay," she said last year in an interview with the National Women's Law Center. "We are determined to resist—fiercely and strategically." Her views test a line between legal advocacy and political activism at a moment when sexual harassment and gender discrimination have become the terrain on which American political warfare is being waged.*

Guess it makes perfect sense, therefore, that this collective of anti-Trumpers would latch on to a story from thirty-six years ago where the main accuser cannot remember any of the major details. These are a few of the total absurdities of the Blasey Ford case; furthermore, who among us cannot remember a truly traumatic event from our childhood? When writing this book I had to recall several events from my childhood, all of which are far less traumatic than alleged violent attempted rape, and yet my ability (with a memory that I would say is average) to recall specific details, including addresses, attendees, and exact sequences or timelines up to twenty years ago, seems far better than Dr. Ford's.

Soon after Blasey Ford emerged, Deborah Ramirez and Julie Swetnick (the latter represented by well-known Democrat swindler and convicted felon Michael Avenatti) also accused Kavanaugh of having exposed himself to them years before. It was at this moment that the word "feminism" took on its truly modern meaning: all men are guilty until proven innocent in a kangaroo court. Blasey Ford and the other Democrat witnesses could have, in one fell swoop, undone a thirty-year legal career: the whole of modern sanity was on trial in Kavanaugh's nomination.

Alleging that Kavanaugh sexually assaulted her in the summer of 1982, Blasey Ford became the ultimate weapon of the liberal feminist movement—soon enough #BelieveAll Women became the mainstream mantra. What an absolute absurdity it is to say #BelieveAllWomen. Do women not lie? Have women never made up a story? Was it not Eve whom the serpent tempted in the Garden of Eden—or was that incident but the earliest fault of the patriarchy?

Women are clearly and evidently as capable of wrongdoing as men. In the spirit of true equality, should we not have our motives questioned as well?

Critics deemed me cynical for not believing a woman who, as a registered Democrat, suddenly felt it appropriate, after thirty years, to come forward to try to discredit one of the most conservative picks for the Supreme Court, by a president who has been universally hated by the Democrats themselves.

So what was in it for Blasey Ford? you might ask. I would say that the $647,610 raised through GoFundMe probably acted as some kind of inspiration, along with the lifelong backing and support of all future aspiring Democrats—indeed, which future Democrat would ever be able to turn down or say no to Christine Blasey Ford, the heroine of the Kavanaugh hearings? The last time I checked, Ford's GoFundMe fund-raiser page had stopped accepting donations, with a message posted that stated, in part, the following:

*The funds you have sent through GoFundMe have been a godsend. Your donations have allowed us to take reasonable steps to protect ourselves against frightening threats, including physical protection and security for me and my family, and to enhance the security for our home. We used your generous contributions to pay for a security service, which began on September 19 and has recently begun to taper off; a home security system; housing and security costs incurred in Washington DC, and local housing for part of the time we have been dis-placed. . . . All funds unused after completion of security expenditures will be donated to organizations that sup-port trauma survivors. I am currently researching orga-nizations where the funds can be best used. We will use this space to let you know when that process is complete.*

It must take many months of research to be able to find those groups, because that was on November 21, 2018, and there has not been an update since. Maybe all those hun-dreds of thousands of dollars seemed too hard to part with after all.

From my standpoint, I watched in awe as liberal femi-nists rallied around Ford as she took the stand in front of the Senate Judiciary Committee to recount the alleged assault. Here was a lynching being conducted in real time for us all to witness, simply on the basis of #BelieveAllWomen, judicial precedent, innocent until proven guilty, the entire premise of our common law system, and the Constitution were put on trial. Had Kavanaugh not been confirmed on the basis of Ford's testimony, the founding premise of the Constitution would have required an amendment that read "We hold these truths to be self-evident, that all men are created equal *under women.*" How entertaining that modern feminists portray themselves as victims from *The Handmaid's Tale* while at the same time working to achieve a legal standing that would have given them such unfettered dominion over the lives of men.

Of course, the whole affair was a sordid degradation of legal process that left me with a sense of unease. Unease at having watched women forcefully demand justice for Ford without a single shred of evidence.

Unease perhaps because, in an effort to stamp out their enemies, modern feminists are drawing upon the most ancient of southern racist tactics.

## "BELIEVE WOMEN" VS. BLACK MEN

Emmett Till was just fourteen when he left his hometown of Chicago to spend the 1955 summer with family in Mississippi. Sadly, he would never make it back home.

While visiting a local grocery store with a group of boys, Till was said to have whistled at Carolyn Bryant, a young white woman who co-owned the store with her husband. It was an unheard-of offense in the Jim Crow South, one that would cost Till his young life.

In the sixty years since Till was ripped from his great-uncle's home, beaten, mutilated, shot, and thrown into the Tallahatchie River with a seventy-pound fan tied around his neck, the exact events that did or did not transpire inside that store remain unclear. Till was accused of whistling at Bryant in an attempt to flirt with her. His mother would later say that her son stuttered and used whistling as a device to help him better pronounce certain words. What is clear, however, is the statement that Bryant made during the trial on behalf of the two men who were acquitted of—and then later admitted to—Till's murder.

Bryant said that Till grabbed her hand and asked for a date, then slipped his hand around her waist and mentioned that he had had sexual encounters with white women before. The twenty-one-year-old said she was scared to death.

It was a shocking statement, considering that Till had been warned about the ways of the South by his mother, who had grown up in Mississippi. It was a shocking statement perhaps most of all, because it was not true. In 2007,

Bryant admitted to Timothy Tyson, author of *The Blood of Emmett Till*, that the physical and verbal advances from Till never happened. She also said that she could not remember anything else that may have happened on that hot August day, thereby calling into question whether Till had ever whistled at her at all.

Bryant's admission was a momentous occasion for a black community that was still struggling to make sense of the unspeakable trauma that was inflicted upon Till's young body—a confirmation of what many had always believed to be true. But the damage, of course, was already long done.

For many years, the tragedy of Emmett Till served as a reminder to Americans of the danger of unchecked allegations. Sadly, his case is far from an anomaly. There are countless historical examples of black men who have been wrongly arrested, jailed, or killed because a woman's word was blindly believed. Yet while people on both sides of the political aisle will agree to the horror of past incidents, Democrats are loath to admit that today *all* men (no longer just black men) are in as much danger of being falsely implicated as they were in days past.

Take for example the case of Malik St. Hilaire: Malik was a black man and Division I football player and student at Sacred Heart University when another student, a nineteen-year-old woman named Nikki Yovino, accused him and one of his teammates of sexual assault in the fall of 2016. Yovino claimed that St. Hilaire and his teammate pulled her into a basement bathroom at a house party thrown by the football team. While St. Hilaire and his friend both admitted to having sex with her, Yovino claimed that they forced her into the act.

The next two years were a wild ride of emotion and devastation for the two men. They were kicked off the team, their scholarships were revoked, and they were expelled from school. And this, of course, says nothing about the shame and embarrassment they had to endure as a result of Yovino's claims.

Yovino, meanwhile, was on her own roller coaster. Three months after the initial investigation, she admitted that she had lied to police about the assault because, according to the arrest warrant affidavit, "It was the first thing that came to mind and she did not want to lose [another male student] as a friend and potential boyfriend." Yovino also believed that "when [her potential boyfriend] heard the allegation it would make him angry and sympathetic to her."

Despite her admission, the investigation continued and ultimately went to court, but during a pretrial hearing, Yovino changed her story once again. She went back to her original version of events and stated that she was, in fact, raped. Ultimately, however, Yovino pleaded guilty to two counts of second-degree falsely reporting an incident and one count of interfering with police, and was sentenced to one year in prison.

Judge William Holden, who presided over the trial, did not mince words when he convicted the unapologetic Yovino. "I just hope you spend the time reflecting on what you did," he said. It was an appropriate statement given the events, but as was the case when Carolyn Bryant admitted to lying about what happened between her and a teenaged Emmett Till, considerable irreversible harm had already been inflicted. St. Hilaire made this clear when he made his statement before the judge and jury.

*I went from being a college student to sitting at home being expelled, with no way to clear my name. I just hope she knows what she has done to me. My life will never be the same. I did nothing wrong, but everything has been altered because of this.*

Yovino's actions so perfectly encapsulate all that reeks about modern feminism.

Something ugly festers beneath the surface of this social

movement, something that makes the Jim Crow–era witch hunts all too relevant again: today we see instances of rape being conflated with instances of shameful regret, and consensual sexual interactions labeled as assaults. In the process, we watch good men smeared by the court of public opinion, their reputations permanently marred.

Jeremiah Harvey was only nine years old when he was accused of touching fifty-three-year-old Teresa Sue Klein inappropriately. They were in a Brooklyn bodega at the same time in the fall of 2018; Harvey was shopping with his mother and younger sister when his backpack brushed Klein's backside as he walked past. Klein felt the contact and immediately assumed predatory intent. "That's right. Her son grabbed my a—," Klein told a 911 operator. "And [then his mother] decided to yell at me. There are security cameras in this bodega," she further indicated.

Klein was right about the cameras in the bodega. She was wrong, however, about Harvey's actions, and the camera footage immediately disproved her claims. With no charges to file, Klein apologized to Harvey but as always is the case, the damage had already been done. Harvey was humiliated by Klein's outburst and accusation, and further traumatized by the concept of his arrest for an offense he never committed.

## FEMINISM, FOR WHOM?

In my travels across the country, liberal women often tell me that I would have nothing if it weren't for feminism. They are shocked at my refusal to accept the "feminist" branding. I too am shocked, but only by their "all-inclusive" reimagining of what the first-wave feminist movement was all about.

Despite the popularization of the modern phrase "feminism is for everybody," it clearly is not for men or for conservative women today, and it certainly was not for black women in the past.

Segregation produced psychological changes. The savage pursuit of black men in the South on the mere basis of an allegation can be largely attributed to the operating belief at that time that white women were vessels of purity; they were to be protected at all costs, especially against the savage instincts of black men who (by their view) would naturally look to defile them. It was deemed a grave sin for a black man to even look at a white woman with interest, graver still if he ever worked up the nerve to touch her. And it was white men—southern Democrats and their Dixiecrat descendants in particular—who committed themselves to ensuring that such sins against their women were never committed, lest the perpetrator wish to play Russian roulette with his own life.

Of course, black women were never held in such high societal regard in those early days. Even in instances when white men were known to have raped or assaulted black women, they were rarely, if ever, held accountable for it. The natural result was that with time, white women— even those who deemed themselves to be "progressive" or "allies"—subconsciously began investing in the concept that they were better than, and somehow separate from, black women.

After the Civil War and through the Reconstruction period, newly freed black Americans began the long-haul battle for equal rights under the law, with the aforementioned support of the Republicans. Black women began engaging politically in the lobbying effort for suffrage. They understood that real power would come only with their right to vote, granting them the ability to elect leaders with their interests in mind. And although some decried the idea that black men might be given the right to vote before them, other black women understood the greater focus should be on the advancements of their community as a whole. They were happy to place the primary focus on the effort for black male suffrage, because unlike white women whose husbands, fathers, and brothers had always held political power, black women had no one to cast a ballot on their behalf.

The set of challenges facing black women was therefore unique and required thoughtful strategy, as Republican Party leaders feared that pushing too forcefully for women's suffrage might indirectly hamper their efforts to enfranchise black men.

Suffragists like Susan B. Anthony, though purportedly committed to racial equality, disagreed vehemently with the notion that white women should have to wait until after black men for their right to vote. In the end, the women's movement resolved to split, with white suffragists distancing themselves from black women whose advocacy was tied to the black community at large. Ultimately, this worked in favor of white suffragists; southern Democrats would more readily consider their push for women's enfranchisement if they needn't worry about consequential black empowerment.

Rebecca Latimer Felton was a vocal advocate for women's rights, a prominent member of the women's suffrage and progressive movements, and the first woman to serve in the U.S. Senate. She was also an unapologetic racist, who held deep notions of white supremacy. Felton believed that no black person, man or woman, should ever be granted the right to vote, a view likely attributable to the fact that the Georgia resident and her husband owned slaves. Never dialed into her own hypocrisy, Felton's suffragist approach was to openly criticize southern men for failing to protect their wives and daughters by ensuring their equal rights. Her calls for equality were somehow separate from her belief that the lynching of blacks was a necessary way to protect oppressed white women. "If it needs lynching to protect woman's dearest possession from the ravening human beasts," Felton said in August 1897, "then I say lynch, a thousand times a week if necessary."

Modern feminists may not believe they have much in common with their racist forebears, but I'd beg to differ. Like their ancestors before them, their interest in the fight for equality extends only as far as their political aspirations.

## A FRIEND OF THE LIBERAL FEMINIST MOVEMENT IS NO FRIEND OF THE BLACK COMMUNITY

To black America, I simply ask that we consider liberal feminism in this truer context of our history. Because this increasingly radical demand for by-any-means feminism seems to me to be but a self-serving ploy by progressives in their all-too-familiar pursuit of power.

Movements like #MeToo provide little more than political advocacy for their wealthy liberal sponsors. Actress Jane Fonda acknowledged the inherent privilege of the movement in an episode of *All In with Chris Hayes* back in October 2017. Speculating as to why #MeToo had suddenly gained so much momentum, she remarked that it was "too bad that it's probably because so many of the women that were assaulted by Harvey Weinstein are famous and white and everybody knows them. This has been going on a long time to black women and other women of color and doesn't get out quite the same."

Though conceding that black women were largely being left out of the conversation, Fonda later remarked that she believed the movement had the potential to effect real change in the lives of all women. "It feels different," she said. "It feels like something has shifted."

But my question is: Whom has it shifted for?

With phrases like "toxic masculinity" and coordinated witch hunts at the drop of an allegation, the apparent goal of feminism seems to be to remove the concept of masculinity from the Western world entirely, making all expressions of manhood obsolete, and all expressions of womanhood guiltless.

The bigger issue is that if manhood becomes obsolete, so too will the family unit. And as we've already discussed, when our dependency on family decreases, our dependency on government increases tenfold.

For black America this hypothesis has been tested affirmatively and conclusively. Truly, no friend of black America is an ally of this perversion of a feminist movement.

# 4

# ON OVERCIVILIZATION

Ruby Bridges was just two months shy of her sixth birthday on November 14, 1960, when she became the first black student to attend the all-white William Frantz Elementary School in New Orleans, Louisiana. As a first grader, she did not understand the gravity of this simple action, nor could she even begin to comprehend its watershed implications, which would come to forever be remembered in the pages of American history. During an interview with *PBS NewsHour* thirty-six years later, Bridges remarked that her parents had intentionally kept many of the particulars of that occasion a secret, a decision that Bridges was ultimately thankful for.

"It would have been very frightening for me as a six-year-old to hear what I might actually see once I got there," she said in 1997. "Driving up I could see the crowd, but living in New Orleans, I actually thought it was Mardi Gras. There was a large crowd of people outside of the school. They were throwing things and shouting, and that sort of goes on in New Orleans at Mardi Gras."

As oblivious as Bridges may have been while outside of Frantz Elementary, her experiences inside the building quickly brought things into stunning perspective. One by one, white parents removed their children from the school and a majority of the teachers resigned in similar protest. There was just one teacher who agreed to teach Bridges—a woman from Boston, Massachusetts, named Barbara Henry. With the remaining white students safely quarantined in other classrooms, Bridges became Mrs. Henry's sole student. With time, the initial pandemonium died down and the angry mob of protestors dwindled. And though rather ironically still somewhat segregated within her own classroom, Ruby finished out the remainder of the school year, forever cementing her status as a cultural icon of integration.

November 2020 will mark the sixtieth anniversary of Bridges's pioneering efforts, and for the first time in decades there is a debate surrounding black integration again—and it is not coming from white people. Today, some black people are *choosing* their segregation, as a token of their own self-empowerment. Suffice to say that not even in the wildest dreams or the darkest nightmares of our ancestors could this predicament have been imagined,

Take the case of Williams College, for example. In November 2018, the black student union held a town hall for "students, particularly black students, to reflect on recent events and the general student experience here" and "to voice concerns and work towards solutions." Of most pressing concern during this town hall was the purported "tokenization" of black students in mostly white spaces, or more specifically, the idea that first-year students felt burdened by the process of acclimating themselves to the white institution. Their proposed solution? Affinity housing or dorms that would accept black students only. Remarkably, these students believed the way to address the issue of their discomfort was by segregating themselves from the rest of the student body—by choice. Not because they *had* to, but because they *wanted* to.

In April 2019, the school newspaper, the *Williams Record*, printed a full editorial board endorsement of the proposal:

*We at the Record wholeheartedly support establish-*
*ing affinity housing at the College. As a community,*
*we must recognize that the College is a predominantly*
*white institution in which students of color often feel*
*tokenized, both in their residences and more broadly on*
*campus. Establishing affinity housing will not single-*
*handedly solve this problem, but it will assist in making*
*the College a more welcoming, supportive and safe com-*
*munity for minoritized students.*

*Some say affinity housing reinforces division, ar-*
*guing that having minoritized students cluster in one*
*space would be harmful to the broader campus com-*
*munity. We believe, however, that allowing for a space*
*where students can express their identities without fear*
*of tokenization or marginalization will encourage stu-*
*dents to exist more freely in the broader campus com-*
*munity, rather than recede from it.*

The editor's insinuation that supporting segregation was
a matter of community safety very closely mirrors the same
arguments made by Americans who were in support of the
Jim Crow laws. Apparently, the broad characterization of
policy decisions as necessary to community safety frees
those who make such sweeping statements from any burden

of having to prove their claims. Of course, there were no purported instances of black students' at Williams College being physically harmed or otherwise threatened by the mere presence of white people.

While the efforts of campus segregation stand in extraordinarily stark contrast to the accomplishments made by six-year-old Ruby Bridges, I cannot feign surprise. I have witnessed firsthand what a disastrous state our college campuses are in; they are little more than social justice camps, coddling the minds of students through trained sensitivities.

It would certainly seem that America has come a long way since 1960—so far, in fact, that we may actually be returning to the place from whence we came. After decades of civil rights crusades, we have perhaps become so accustomed to fighting for progress that we are pushing it to the point of our own detriment. The truth is that black America currently finds itself in a position of privilege that civil rights leaders of the 1960s could only have dreamed. Yet rather than bask in the glory of our victories, we are instead creating new challenges.

All of these developments reflect the current social climate of America, which I have come to describe as "over-civilized."

## THE TREND TOWARD OVERCIVILIZATION

For all the strides we have made to get to where we are in American society today, progress did not arrive without extended periods of immorality—or periods of undercivilization. Human slavery, segregation, Japanese internment camps—these are all occurrences when civility was lacking and in desperate need of progressive reform. When called to we made the necessary changes to improve our society, and it is evident that our country's worst days are far behind us. Unfortunately, not all nations can make the same claim. There are still live slave auctions in Libya, where migrants find themselves trafficked into forced labor and prostitution. And rather extraordinarily, in Malawi, albinos are kidnapped and sacrificed to witch doctors so that their body parts can be used for rituals designed to help politicians win their seats during general elections. Despite these horrific conditions, steps are being made toward progress; human trafficking and humanitarian aid groups are on the ground daily, working to improve the quality of life for people all over the world.

The desire and ability to progress over time is an inextricable part of our humanity. It is the reason that every civilization since the dawn of time has constantly sought improvement via innovation, scientific discovery, and philo-sophical debate. But what happens when civil maturity is realized, when basic rights and liberties have been ensured for all? What does a society strive toward then?

The answer is what I believe might be plaguing America today: overcivilization.

Civilization was achieved when we made the decision as a country to welcome law-abiding immigrants from around the world into our lands, while also providing due process for those seeking asylum from less civilized circumstances. But overcivilization is what is happening now via Democrat politicians' demands that we become a country with no borders—allowing any and every undocumented person to flood into our lands.

Civilization was achieved for gay couples in the United States when the Supreme Court ruled in favor of same-sex marriage in 2015. Overcivilization, however, is the LGBTQ community's current quest for transgender rights, or, more accurately described, the demand that biological men who self-identify as women be granted legal permission to use ladies' restrooms and dominate women's sports competitions.

We reached civilization within the black community when we received our rights to live, work, vote, and love in accordance with our own desires. Overcivilization is our current state of race-baiting, fabricated oppression, and calls for self-imposed segregation.

The absurdity of our circumstances has led me to contemplate whether peace might be an unnatural state for humanity. It's why I often credit my generation, the millennials, for having turned our country into a whiny cesspool of neoliberalism. Let's face it, those born in America after the 1980s are among the most privileged human beings ever to walk the face of the planet. And yet spending hours daily on our smartphones and rotating between various social media apps seems to have left us devoid of contentment. Our desire for a more meaningful existence has driven us to the never-ending pursuit of "social justice" causes: causes like gender-neutral bathroom signs, and proper pronouns available for those struggling with their identity. Indeed, only in a time of tremendous peace can such meaninglessness banter take place.

Our understanding of what it means to experience hardship has been warped by a prolonged period of goodness. The generation before us lived through the Vietnam War, which the United States combat forces participated in for seventeen grueling years. And just fourteen short years before the start of that conflict, young American men who should have been enrolling in college were instead enlisting in what would come to be known as the bloodiest conflict in human history: World War II. And just a little more than two decades before then marked the start of World War I, battles fought among men whose average age was twenty-four but reached as low as just twelve years. Fast-forward to today and students are demanding safe spaces on college campuses because they view it as a form of torture to be exposed to opposing viewpoints.

Yes, in the wake of achieving progress, in the manifestation phase of our ancestors' dreams, we are now working overtime to dismantle all that they fought for.

We have no world wars to end, no major civil rights issues to champion, and yet our desire to triumph rages on. It would appear that we love an underdog story so much so that we are now unnecessarily casting ourselves as underdogs.

Of course, there is danger in this pursuit past the point of civilization. For it is possible to demand so much progress that regression is the natural result.

## PLAYING THE RACE CARD—AND LOSING

When twelve-year-old Amari Allen claimed in September 2019 that three of her white male classmates at Immanuel

Christian School in Springfield, Virginia, had pinned her down and forcefully cut her dreadlocks, the liberal community quickly gathered in a collective rage. "They were saying that I don't deserve to live, that I shouldn't have been born," Allen said. She went on to explain in great detail how the boys held her hands behind her back and covered her mouth while they cut her hair with scissors, calling it "ugly" and "nappy."

In the midst of a recent debate about black boys being excluded from sports for hairstyles deemed "inappropriate," Allen's story represented the icing on a perfectly baked media cake of white supremacy. It was tangible evidence that racism still permeates the lives of black children.

Left-wing networks immediately got behind the story. As a rule, they deem all stories of racial prejudice irresistible, but this particular story bore an unusual strand of novelty. As it would turn out, Allen's school was already familiar to the press. Familiar not only because it had made national news the previous January for a circulated parental agreement that stipulated that the administration reserves the right to expel students on the basis of promoting homosexual or bisexual activities (a typical guideline for religious schools)—but also because Immanuel Christian School employed Karen Pence, the art-teaching wife of Vice President

Mike Pence. Naturally, every obsessed anti-Trump major media outlet, from CNN to CBS to the *New York Times*, was desperate to cover Allen's hate crime. Reporters first castigated the school as a whole for allowing such a heinous crime to take place in the first place; they then moved to casting doubt on the credibility of a Christian education altogether; and then, of course, they used the Second Lady's connection to the school to drive home their ultimate point, of a racist, bigoted Trump administration.

There was only one problem with Allen's story, albeit a pretty big one: it never happened. As investigations into the attack got under way, security footage from the school revealed discrepancies in her initial account. When questioned about the inconsistencies, Allen finally admitted that she had fabricated the event.

The irresponsibility of her fabrication cannot be overstated. In her desire to be cast as a victim, Allen's claim furthered the media-driven divide between black and white Americans, the former further convinced that they cannot live safely because of the color of their skin, the latter likely growing fatigued with another false-flag operation executed at their expense.

It was not so long ago that a fifteen-year-old girl named Tawana Brawley caused a similar fiasco, accusing four white men of raping her, tearing her clothes, writing racial slurs on her body, and smearing her with feces. The case stoked a media firestorm when the always-combative Al Sharpton began advising Brawley, fanning the flames of racial unrest. A number of black celebrities came out in support of the teenager: Bill Cosby offered a $25,000 reward for any information about the case, Don King pledged $100,000 toward her future education, and Mike Tyson gifted her with a watch valued at $30,000 to express his sympathy. Rather unfortunately for them, Brawley's story didn't check out. Soon after her attorneys dramatically named New York police officers and a prosecuting attorney as suspects, a grand jury determined that the attack was staged by Brawley herself, likely to avoid punishment from her stepfather for staying out past her curfew. "I had to sit down with my daughters and explain to them that this was a case where someone made reckless allegations," accused attorney Steven Pagones told the *New York Post* in 2012. "It didn't ruin me, but it certainly had a huge impact on every aspect of my life."

Nearly twenty years later, in 2006, another scandal rocked the nation, when at the Duke University campus three members of the men's lacrosse team were accused of rape. Crystal Gail Mangum, a black woman who attended a nearby university and worked part-time as a stripper, was hired to perform at an off-campus party hosted by the lacrosse team. Tensions between the team and the entertainment cut the party short, leading to Mangum's early departure along with a woman who was hired to work the party with her. Soon after, the two women began arguing in a car, and when Mangum refused to exit the other woman's vehicle, she was taken into police custody. Mangum was severely impaired, and while being involuntarily admitted to a mental health and substance-abuse facility, and while likely hoping to evade further trouble, she began spinning the tale of her rape.

The resulting fallout was tremendous. The alleged rape was deemed a hate crime. In early April, the team's coach was forced to resign and Duke's president canceled the remaining games of the 2006 season. Prosecutors soon learned that Mangum—who is now serving time in a Goldsboro, North Carolina, prison for an unrelated murder conviction—had been untruthful. In April 2007, all charges were dropped, declaring all three of the accused lacrosse players innocent.

But the social pollution from false allegations lingers long after the truth is revealed. In an article titled "The Cautionary Tale of Amari Allen," Tom Ascol, the president of Founders Ministries, addressed the Allen controversy and what it said about the current state of our society:

> *We live in a hyper-racialized culture that undermines real racial harmony. Those who insist that every offense or slight that takes place as well as every inequity that exists between racially diverse people is necessarily due to racial injustice contribute to this combustible situation. All injustice is due to sin but not all injustice is due to sinful partiality. But when racism is redefined in terms of post-modern power structure formulas, then every failure of those impugned with "whiteness" is attributed to racial injustice.*

To say that racial harmony is being undermined is an understatement. Our media pounces at every chance to cover discrimination because the Ghost of Racism Past has proven to be a profitable model. With money as their motive, I suspect they give little thought to what their negativity has inspired among the black youth. They must disregard entirely the fact that their fevered coverage is leading some to spin wild tales in a quest to live up to the hype of their own perceived oppression, while others experiment with self-imposed segregation. And in the process, the relationship between white and black Americans continues to fray, neither group benefiting from the resulting distance between each other. Despite the current trends and discussions, there is absolutely no proof that black Americans fare better at achieving, or are by any means safer among our own race. In fact, all evidence points to the contrary.

According to the 2018 Status and Trends in the Education of Racial and Ethnic Groups, nearly 60 percent of black students attend schools in which minorities constitute at least 75 percent of total enrollment.

Despite this, among fourth graders, the reading gap between white and black students was 26 points in 2017, and by the time black students enter high school, they are as far behind white students as they were twenty-five years earlier. In math, the gap between white and black students was 25 points in 2017. Black eighth graders were a full 32 points behind their white peers, another nearly identical statistic from decades earlier. When I think about these troubling statistics, I cannot help but think about Amari Allen and the wonderful opportunity she was given to attend an elite private school like Immanuel Christian, an opportunity most black girls her age are never afforded. And I can't help but consider that despite the fact that her parents paid $12,000 per year to afford her that unique opportunity, she risked it all to lie about racism.

The idea that blacks fare better among other blacks is disproven not only by looking at our trailing academic performance, but also by the failure of most black inner-city neighborhoods; without question, our neighborhoods rank as the most unsafe in the country. The residents of the late Elijah Cummings's district in Baltimore are certainly not benefiting simply because their community leaders are all black. Despite being represented by a black congressman, their neighborhood streets are littered with trash, empty buildings, and rodents scurrying between. The abandoned buildings, high crime rates, and plummeting home values paint a picture all too familiar to black communities that are run by black Democrats. Like Flint, Michigan, like Newark, New Jersey—communities run by left-wing politicians struggle to have even their most basic infrastructural needs met.

And while much hubbub has been created about the reasons that contribute to these circumstances, few dare point out the irony: liberal black Americans cry out often about the fear of white men, yet can claim no solace in predominately black spaces.

## THE RACIST BOOGEYMAN

There is an endless stream of faux outrage, a constant manufacturing of nonexistent hurdles, rooted in some flawed concept of our society's perfectibility. There are those in black America who use charges of racism as a social handicap. With the expectation that the mere utterance of the word will vindicate them in every scenario, we have arrived suddenly into an era of more insistence on rather than actual resistance against racism. And the Left, always happy to exploit our victimhood, urges us on. Many times, in fact, white liberals join in on the game, alleging that they see instances of discrimination and microaggressions everywhere, as proof of their commitment to our cause.

The personality complex of a liberal savior is one that fascinates me, as I believe it to be centered on extreme narcissism. I imagine them to be addicted to the feeling of accomplishment that is derived from helping someone inferior to them. I'd imagine it's something like the feeling most get when they drop off items at Goodwill: a sense of charity, overridden by the more likely fact that they spend in excess of their needs. Standing up for inferior blacks must liberate liberals from having to assess their own flawed characters. Or perhaps, as in the case of Democrat politicians, they will simply say anything to garner our support.

While it is well within reason to remark at injustice, the immediate claim that every moment of our temporary discomfort is due to inherent racism is as insane as suggesting that the solution to such discomfort is segregation. It is impossible to forge ahead while walking backward.

And consider the drama if it were white people who made such recommendations, accusing blacks of racism and calling for separate (but equal!) dormitories to quarantine themselves from such offenses. We would be utterly outraged, so why is our response any different when members of our own community author such proposals? I have given consideration to the idea that recognizing our equality might make some black people uncomfortable, because with no one to blame but ourselves for failures, the weight of our own irresponsibility may seem too heavy a burden to bear. It is much easier to go through life with a white supremacist boogeyman.

And so we become willing participants in the Left's sport of identity politics, despite the perpetual outcome of our defeat. So comforted are we by the ease of the progressive path laid beneath our feet, that we ignore that it's a path to nowhere.

But what would our ancestors think?

What would your grandmother, your great-grandmother, or your great-great-grandmother say if they saw you now? Better yet, what would *you* say if you were transported back to their upbringing, and made to endure the reality of what they lived through to grant you the opportunities that lie just beneath your feet? It was my grandmother's unexpected death that forced me to harvest the seeds of her legacy. My hope is that the thought of your ancestry inspires you to do the same.

Never should we set ourselves on a fruitless quest for an imaginary utopia. Rather, we ought to commit ourselves to the steady remembrance of the sacrifice and hardship that came before us, so that we may appreciate the many blessings of our circumstances today.

# 5

# ON SOCIALISM AND GOVERNMENT HANDOUTS

Human beings have a strange relationship with the truth: we would much rather hear what makes us feel good than a hard-hitting, fundamental fact. I believe this is especially true in the black community. Carrying the burden of generations of oppression has left us longing for goodness—for politicians, media, and others to pander to our delicate emotions rather than deliver any stinging truth regarding our predicament.

The dictionary defines *truth* as "that which is true and in accordance with fact." Truth, then, is universal and absolute. It transcends our humanity, our imperfect societies, and the leaders within them. Two plus two, for example, will always equal four. Upon any continent, within any city, under any leadership, this conclusion will always hold true.

*Goodness*, on the other hand, is less certain; it is defined as "the quality of being morally good." And unlike the factual constraints of truth, goodness is marked by its subjectivity. Indeed, what seems good to you may not seem good to me, and vice versa. Our current circumstances, our past experiences, and our circle of family, friends, and coworkers all help determine our perspective of what we deem good or not.

Inevitably, if you put a handful of people in a room with differing backgrounds, they are bound to disagree. And when they do disagree, lines will be drawn and factions formed as people align themselves with those who seem the most sympathetic to their perspectives. That is a fundamental course in how problems arise.

Take the abortion debate, for example. Pro-choice advocates stand on the side of the would-be mother and the "goodness" of supporting her right to decide whether she should carry a fetus to term once she becomes pregnant. Despite liberal points to the contrary, the question at the center of the debate is not about whether an early pregnancy constitutes life (the demand for the procedure itself reveals an understanding that even at the point of conception, the fetus is a living thing that will grow, as only living things can do). The argument between pro-choicers and pro-lifers, then, is not about science or what is *true*—it is about an individual's idea of what is *good*.

In our current social climate in which activists and politicians can turn something as fundamental as life itself into a matter of subjectivity, promising to do "good" is the platform of many political leaders. And when dealing with the black community, the concept of "goodness" has become synonymous with "free stuff."

Right now, Democrat candidates are attempting to shore up black votes by detailing what they will give us if elected. And I might be offended if I didn't see the humor of this repeat tragedy. Truly, this old dog is learning no new tricks. Lest we forget, Democrats first lured blacks away from the Republican Party via the same routine—the promise that goverment intervention would significantly improve our livelihood. But for the Democrat establishment, promises made are problems kept. By all serious economic retro-assessments, Franklin Delano Roosevelt's "New Deal" was an absolute disaster. In fact, a 2004 analysis concluded that government interventions prolonged the Great Depression by several years. This conclusion is supported by the fact that in the first year following the stock market crash of 1929, absent any federal intervention, "unemployment peaked at 9 percent, two months after the [crash] and began drifting downward until it reached 6.3 percent in June of 1930. That was when the federal government made its first major intervention with the Smoot-Hawley tariff. After . . . unemployment rates reversed and shot up . . . within six months, unemployment reached double digits at 11.6 percent in November 1930. After a series of additional large federal interventions in the economy, unemployment stayed in the double digits for the remainder of the decade."

Roosevelt's 1933 National Industrial Recovery Act (NIRA) was a critical component of his New Deal plan to put Americans back to work. And in a statement made on June 16, 1933, Roosevelt set the hearts of millions of destitute Americans at ease with his vow to create new income-earning opportunities for those who needed them most:

*Between these twin efforts—public works and industrial reemployment—it is not too much to expect that a great many men and women can be taken from the ranks of the unemployed before winter comes. It is the most important attempt of this kind in history. As in*

*the great crisis of the World War, it puts a whole people*
*to the simple but vital test: "Must we go on in many*
*groping, disorganized, separate units to defeat or shall*
*we move as one great team to victory?"*

It was on this premise that FDR campaigned for votes, promising that even the black men and women who were struggling to keep their heads above water would benefit from his transformative policy. It all sounded "good," but it did not take long for black America to realize that FDR's promises were empty. The NRA was a key tenet of the NIRA, and while it was officially known as the National Recovery Administration, it was eventually given more accurate pseudonyms in the black community, including the "Negro Removal Act," "Negroes Ruined Again," and "Negroes Robbed Again."

The NRA gave previously unprecedented power to unions that refused membership to black workers in most cases. Meanwhile, government mandates for minimum wages kept employers from hiring blacks who were too unskilled to be deemed worthy of the pay increase. What's more, legal guidelines prevented blacks from usurping the unfair hiring practices, because they were not allowed to offer to work for lower wages. Unironically, 1930 is the last year that black unemployment was lower than white unemployment. Federally mandated minimum wage laws did away with that occurrence altogether.

Blacks engaged in agricultural work faced an entirely different set of challenges. In the South, blacks were forced off land that the government began paying landowners to leave unfarmed. The goal was to drive agriculture prices back up to pre–World War I levels by reducing inventory, but the artificial reduction of the market put many black tenant farmers out of work. Sharecroppers were technically entitled to a percentage of a farm's profits, including any government funds that were allocated to acreage reduction. Initially, the federal government sent those funds directly to sharecroppers, but complaints from southern Democrats ended that practice, leaving landless black farmers jobless and incomeless.

What is most surprising about the many ways in which these policies hurt black Americans is that it did nothing to quell their willingness to vote in even larger numbers for Democrats again in 1936—helping Roosevelt cruise to a landslide victory. As it turns out, the black community's support of FDR had little to do with the *truth* that his New Deal policies caused disproportionate harm to the black community and everything to do with the *goodness* that blacks saw in the promises made by his administration. Furthermore, as FDR consistently pandered to racist southern Democrats and refused to rock the congressional boat by introducing legislation that would tackle racism head-on, his wife, Eleanor, presented herself as a sympathetic ear legitimately concerned about the issues facing black Americans.

It was Eleanor who pushed for antilynching legislation (though she knew her husband would never support it) and helped form the black cabinet, a group of people who became "advisors" to the Roosevelt administration on matters affecting the black community (though they were never involved in creating actual policy). Eleanor also befriended well-respected activist and educator Mary McLeod Bethune and arranged for her to become the director of the Division of Negro Affairs of the National Youth Administration. Encouraged by the endorsement of Bethune and other influential blacks, Eleanor became the new face of the Democrat Party, and blacks, sensing sincerity in the First Lady's outspokenness about racism, ignored the fact that her husband, the president, was responsible for making their economic circumstances worse.

Sound familiar?

Right now, as Democrats build out platforms pledging to give black people more stuff—reparations, free health care, student loan forgiveness, free college tuition, etc.—they prey upon the same vulnerabilities and frustrations that Eleanor Roosevelt did with the same tacit understanding that their policies will do nothing to alter the situation. Their strategy is to feign sympathy and friendship, with zero intent of transforming circumstances. Perhaps more worrisome is the fact that their push for government solutions has grown increasingly more ambitious. They now openly advocate for transforming all of America into a socialist state. According to a recent Gallup poll, only 47 percent of Democrats view capitalism favorably, while a mind-blowing 57 percent are in favor of socialism—the abhorrent political system that would abolish private property, transform the government into an all-powerful dictatorship, and otherwise destroy everything great about this country.

But you do not have to take my word on how horrible socialism is, nor do you have to go back to the 1800s to see how socialism has ravaged nations. Right now, in the twenty-first century, countries are still implementing the worst social experiment known to man and ruining the lives of millions of people in the process.

## A BRIEF HISTORY OF SOCIALISM

Socialism is the ultimate example of promised goodness, of a noble benevolence to a society's poor and destitute, and only when great portions of a population have been mercilessly impoverished and slaughtered (typically, the people whom socialism was promised to help) is the truth revealed. I find it truly amazing that socialism is implemented as often as it is, given its history of utter failure. Time and time again, politicians promise different results, but everything always unfolds exactly as it has before. In this sense, socialism is the ultimate example of human insanity as defined by Einstein: doing the same thing over and over again and expecting different results.

Socialism is a parasite, a cancer, a lie. And like all lies, it will eventually kill. It kills the society that gives birth to it, destroying the social fabric and contracts that govern basic day-to-day interactions. It kills families—indeed, in *The Communist Manifesto,* the essential reading on nineteenth-century socialist/communist thought, Karl Marx and Friedrich Engels argued for the explicit "Abolition of the family!" They believed that the traditional family structure was the source of private property and the division of labor, and that the innate nature of humans was to exist in sexually free, open communities.

Socialism kills faith, as all challenges to the supremacy and authority of the state must be abolished, including God. Socialism certainly kills the spirits of entrepreneurism and self-improvement, as all aspiration is stripped from society in an attempt to maintain a state of commonality. And finally, of course, socialism kills people. The saddest outcome of all socialist republics is the starvation, death, and/or forced slaughter of the populace, all done in an attempt to maintain the power of tyrannical leftists and stamp down the inevitable uprisings from the poor and powerless who are made slaves to the socialist system.

For people struggling to make ends meet, who are unemployed and drowning in medical debt, the idea of living in a society in which the government provides all basic needs—food, shelter, health care—sounds appealing. But the realities of socialism never match its grandiose ideals. Only those in power are afforded a "good" life with all of the privileges we now enjoy. Conversely, those on the bottom rungs of society struggle to barely get by—the difference being that they are now prevented from ever moving up life's ladder.

Today there is no greater example of socialism's ills than Venezuela. By any measure, Venezuela represents a modern tragedy, a once-great South American nation now brought to its knees.

After struggling to feed themselves and their families, the people of Venezuela are now engaged in a great exodus, deserting their homeland for countries that offer them the opportunity to simply stay alive. With millions of Venezuelans having already fled the ravaged country, Nicolás Maduro, the current president, announced that he was closing the Venezuela–Brazil border, in part to prevent the entry of humanitarian aid in what was deemed a foreign "provocation." While the decision was later overturned by the supreme court, the reopening of the Brazilian border provided little hope for Venezuelans seeking relief. This is, indeed, one of the great ironies of socialism: while capitalists are accused of building walls to keep people out, socialists build walls to keep people in.

Meanwhile, as is so often the case for socialist countries, the transfer of power back to Venezuelan citizens has become nearly impossible. Maduro assumed his presidential post via what many foreign governments believe was a rigged election; soon after, the congress granted Maduro the ability to rule by decree, effectively forming a government of absolutism that allows the president to pass laws without congressional approval. Since this happened in 2013, Maduro has used his powers to effectively trample on the rights of individuals without fear of ramification, and private property, the old enemy of the socialist, has been seized by the government. In the same year that Maduro was allowed to rule by decree, private business owners were arrested and accused of speculating and hoarding, while government-mandated prices on goods led to mass destocking of inventory with no incentive for businesses to restock. At the same time, skyrocketing inflation that occurred as a result of the government printing excess money has led to chronic currency devaluation. In fact, the hyperinflation led Maduro to institute a new currency in 2018, the bolívar soberano, though it still has not remedied Venezuela's inflation issues.

So what does this mean, in practice? What would happen if socialism-induced hyperinflation took over the United States? For starters, the dollar bill would become worthless almost overnight, the hundred-dollar bill insignificant inside of a month. At the same time, the price of your morning cup of coffee would double on a daily basis, while the cost of your weekly visit to the grocery store would quadruple within a week. Moreover, that weekly shopping trip would become physically impossible, as the amount of cash you would have to lug around—bags and bags full—to make said purchases would be too much for the average person to bear.

This is socialism manifest—economic catastrophe caused by price controls, blowout debt, poor management of government industries, and the nationalization of efficient private businesses. The end result? Death, starvation, and mass emigration. Maduro, living in the presidential palace in Caracas, the capital of Venezuela, continues to ignore the worsening plight of the people he claims to represent. Meanwhile, President Trump spoke absolute truth when he said, "The problem in Venezuela is not that socialism has been poorly implemented, but that socialism has been faithfully implemented."

Former British prime minister Margaret Thatcher, an avowed antisocialist, noted, "Socialists cry, 'Power to the people' and raise the clenched fist as they say it. We all know what they mean—power over people, power to the State." Yet the fact remains that politicians around the world, including the United States, still view socialism as an aspirational, utopian ideal. In America, as Democrat leaders continue to brainwash people with their socialist rhetoric, they rely on distressed minorities—particularly blacks—to support this narrative. And there is no one guiltier of this manipulation than Congresswoman Alexandria Ocasio-Cortez.

———

Comparisons have often been drawn between myself and AOC, the young Latina socialist from New York City. On the surface, these comparisons are fair; we were born in the same year, and we are fellow minority women with large social media followings. However, we have arrived at radically opposed political conclusions. She and I perhaps illustrate the war of ideas that presently rages within Western societies, and while Ocasio-Cortez has chosen the pursuit of goodness, I have chosen the path of truth.

Like all socialists who came before her, Ocasio-Cortez appears to rely on class warfare—a struggle between the haves and have-nots—to justify the need for her existence and the power of the Left. Helplessness, then, becomes a necessary ingredient to maintain power. She is certainly consistent in her socialist crusade, even taking actions that seem to work directly against the interests of the district she represents in Congress. Case in point: When Amazon announced in 2018 that it had plans to build its second national headquarters in New York City, Ocasio-Cortez

rallied her constituents and some of the city's liberal opinion leaders against the deal.

Understand, this deal would have brought with it
25,000–40,000 new jobs to the city, as well as at least $30
billion in revenue. What is more, the headquarters were
not set to be in Manhattan, where there is already concen-
trated wealth. They were to be built in Long Island City, a
working-class area in an outer borough that is struggling
economically. According to statistics from the New York
City Community Health District last taken in 2015, 19
percent of the population in Long Island City lives below
the federal poverty level, and unemployment is hovering at
a higher-than-the-national-average 9 percent. Adding insult
to the injury inflicted by the Latina AOC, Long Island City
and next-door Astoria are 28 percent Hispanic (with 41
percent of the population having limited English profi-
ciency) and about 10 percent black.

Clearly, this was a community that needed the massive
influx of revenue, jobs, and prosperity that an Amazon
headquarters would have provided. But the congresswoman
revolted against the promised tax breaks to the business and
accused the company of being morally deficient when
choosing the city as its home. In a series of tweets, AOC
blasted the proposed deal, claiming that her residents were

more concerned about the deterioration of New York subways than they were having *jobs*. "It's possible to establish economic partnerships [with] real opportunities for working families, instead of a race to the bottom competition," she tweeted. She then continued her assault, adding, "while there isn't enough money for hot water in NYCHA, we're giving $3 billion away to Amazon."

Her attack was entirely senseless. Under no circumstances was any of New York's budget going to be redirected to Amazon; that simply is not how a tax break works. But if the Amazon ordeal is any indication, it seems to me that the truth does not matter to Ocasio-Cortez. Not when she espouses the virtues of socialism, nor when she manipulates her millions of Twitter followers by playing to their deepest fears. AOC relied on the ignorance—or, more accurately, the unsophistication—of the working class regarding complex municipal tax incentives to inspire their outrage, while making herself appear to be a moral hero in the process. The confusion and mass hysteria she inspired were enough to make Amazon temporarily pull out of the deal.

In the aftermath, AOC celebrated her first major win as a socialist congresswoman. But her victory was not over Amazon. AOC defeated the truth, and she defeated the millions of people who stood in agreement with her fallacious arguments simply because she claimed to be doing good by fighting the bad of capitalism. Even now, as Amazon has come back to the table and agreed to expand its New York operations by taking out a 335,000-square-foot lease in the city, the truth remains concealed. The fact remains that not only are the 1,500 positions that will be housed in the new space a far cry from the number of new jobs initially promised, but the new Amazon office is planned for Manhattan's Hudson Yards—in the same neighborhood where Facebook recently made a giant footprint. It is a neighborhood that is scarcely in need of development and a neighborhood that, while physically being only four miles from Long Island City, is conceptually light-years away from the black community that would have most benefited from Amazon's initial development plans.

## SELF-SUFFICIENCY IS THE KEY TO BLACK SUCCESS

More than any other group in this country, blacks have had to place an unnatural amount of faith in the American government. We needed the government to free us from the shackles of slavery, to afford us our right to vote, and to grant us the same rights and privileges as white citizens. Somewhere in the process, I fear we began to worship government, to believe that its benevolence is our only source of promise. We have been preconditioned to fall easily for the socialist trap, preset to believe the foolish lies of socialist leaders, like AOC and Bernie Sanders. We have forgotten, perhaps, that the same government that freed us from bondage is the one that bound us in the first place.

Is it not ironic that a community of people who were at first enslaved by government policies, then segregated by government policies, and over the last six decades have been systematically destroyed by government policies, somehow believes that more government might offer a solution to their circumstances? Logically, any attempt at government expansion should be vehemently opposed by the black community. Based on our history, we should be on the front lines of the fight against socialism, and yet the Left's promise of more charity continues to prove irresistible. Our internal conflict is understandable—why shouldn't the government, after years of slavery and Jim Crow, not eliminate black debt by subsidizing black housing, and otherwise funding black lives? The answer is simple: because a painkiller cannot eliminate cancer. No short-term fix, no Band-Aid over the deeply infected wound, will ever fix the underlying problems that plague our community. As Margaret Thatcher famously said, "Socialist governments traditionally do make a financial mess. They always run out of other people's money." No matter how much money the government gives to black America, it would be taking it from somewhere else, and those funds will eventually run out. This wealth distribution is achieved via taxation, and as Winston Churchill, who served as British prime minister during World War II, said, "for a nation to try to tax itself into prosperity is like a man standing in a bucket and trying to lift himself up by the handle."

What is more, when the funds do run dry, blacks, having never learned how the dollars were earned, will be left in the position of once again needing to beg the government for survival. Handouts absent hard work render men weak, and with depleted self-esteem; they stifle the entrepreneurial spirit, by removing our innate senses of drive and aspiration. Poverty and despair become the life of the man who is given a fish but never learns to cast his own line. And though many will sympathize, prosperity will never be won until we become our own lifeline.

The three decades from 1900 to 1930, dubbed the Golden Age of Black Business, lend credence to my claim that we can do it without assistance. It was a period when tens of thousands of black men and women took their economic destinies into their own hands by launching companies. With racist policies barring blacks from many jobs and suitable wage, and with no reasonable hope for government intervention, blacks had to do for themselves. And they did.

In 1900, Booker T. Washington launched the National Negro Business League to provide a network of support for black entrepreneurs with the goal of promoting "commercial and financial development of the Negro." For Washington, it was clear that this path was the only one that would ultimately lead to true equality for the race. During his last annual address to the league before his death, he stated, "At the bottom of education, at the bottom of politics, even at the bottom of religion itself there must be for our race, as for all races an economic foundation, economic prosperity, economic independence."

From 1900 to 1914, the number of black businesses doubled from 20,000 to 40,000, but by 1929 the country had fallen into the Great Depression, and blacks, especially, struggled to break free. But while it is understandable that the black community turned to government assistance in those impossibly lean years, it is confounding that retrospect hasn't taught us any lessons.

Black America will never become prosperous via welfare and government handouts; if it were possible, it would have already happened.

For too long we have been misled by Democrats, who have depended upon our votes for power. For too long we have been made to believe that the state is sovereign, that we cannot lead prosperous lives without assistance from the government. But the truth is that we do not belong to the Democrat Party, nor do we belong to their socialist creed. We answer not to the false god of government, but to the one true God of our faith. Socialism *is* the gospel of envy and the sharing of misery, and our time within the pages of its history is coming to an end.

# 6

# ON EDUCATION

Consider the word "free" for a moment and record what images flash across your mind. When I do this exercise, I picture a young woman in an open field: eyes closed, curly hair hanging loosely, with her face tilted toward the sun. You may have conjured up an entirely different illustration, but suffice to say that the concept of freedom induces positive thoughts.

We most certainly do not correlate the word with our various responsibilities. "Free" is hardly considered in the context of our chores. And yet, that is precisely what freedom entails: personal responsibility.

In a truly free society, individuals are granted responsibility for themselves. Freedom necessitates that we learn how to provide for ourselves, contributing value in whatever form, to generate personal income. We then decide how we wish to spend or save earned income; freedom is the reward for fulfilling personal responsibilities.

Conversely, slavery is the ultimate example of removing personal responsibility. Slaves were prevented from assuming any obligations to themselves; they could not create for themselves, enjoy the fruits of their labor, or prepare for their futures in any way.

One year after passing the Civil Rights Act of 1964, Lyndon B. Johnson gave a historic commencement address to Howard University, where he asserted:

> *Freedom is the right to share, share fully and equally, in American society—to vote, to hold a job, to enter a public place, to go to school. It is the right to be treated in every part of our national life as a person equal in dignity and promise to all others.*

He was correct. Prior to the abolishment of Jim Crow laws, black Americans had never been granted true freedom. Segregation made it so that we were still oppressed through various limitations. Blacks were not free to choose where to educate themselves, where to live, or even whom to socialize with. Unfortunately, however, LBJ continued his address by stating, "But freedom is not enough. You do not wipe away the scars of centuries by saying, 'Now you are free to go where you want, and do as you desire, and choose the leaders you please.'"

Here he is wrong. Dangerously wrong. Being freed *was* enough for black America. The year 1964 should have represented a new beginning, when we began assuming full responsibility over our own lives. It should have marked a period when we made the extra effort to close the gap that the years of oppression had created between us and white America. What black Americans needed in 1964, more than anything, was a commitment to education. The only available means for us to close the gap on the many areas that we lagged was through an exertion of hard work and study.

Against this reality the president who granted us our rights told us, within the same breath, that we needed help from white Americans to get ahead. Miraculously, just as soon as we were given personal responsibility, it was taken away. In the darkest of ironies, after 345 years of having our personal responsibility stripped from us by governing white society, we allowed that same white society to take it right back. Their method for taking it had certainly changed. Rather than callously telling us we *couldn't* be responsible for ourselves, by outwardly barring and banning us from various institutions, this time, they began telling us we *shouldn't* be responsible for ourselves because it was unimaginable that blacks would suddenly be expected to perform at their level. This ushered in a period of black victimization, which our community readily embraces to this day.

To be clear, the belief that white people are to assume all responsibility for black America's shortcomings is a form of white power. One must believe in black inferiority to accept the thesis that black America is not responsible for any of its own shortcomings in a free society. Conservatives believe neither in white power nor black inferiority, which is why we routinely reject the narrative that the white man is to blame for all of our ills.

Black Americans who do accept this narrative do so not because they are "woke" but because they are terrified. They are terrified to accept responsibility for their own lives. This deep-seated fear is exactly what spawned the period of black militancy that began just after the passage of the Civil Rights Act. At the very moment they were freed, blacks of that era recognized the burden of freedom, and began searching for something to excuse their many shortcomings. And LBJ, in that momentous commencement address, delivered it to them. Now blacks learned that even if they were free, they could still be victims.

Shelby Steele, a black American conservative author who grew up during this period, describes this phenomenon:

*The greatest black problem in America today is freedom. All underdeveloped, formerly oppressed groups first experience new freedom as a shock and a humiliation, because freedom shows them their underdevelopment and their inability to compete as equals. Freedom seems to confirm all the ugly stereotypes about the group—especially the charge of inferiority—and yet the group no longer had the excuse of oppression. Without oppression—the group automatically becomes responsible for its inferiority and non-competitiveness. So freedom not only comes as a humiliation but also as an overwhelming burden of responsibility.*

*(from* White Guilt, *Harper Collins, 2006, p. 67)*

There is nothing more terrifying than freedom, particularly when it arrives to you suddenly, after years of oppression. After years of being told that they were unequal, black Americans suddenly had to contend with the empirical proof that indeed they were, albeit through no fault of their own. Understandably, due to prior oppression, blacks lagged greatly behind white Americans in all areas of education. Too fearful to rise to the challenge of outworking our opponents, we accepted the poison of the victim narrative that we see today. Rather than dealing with the burden of responsibility, we began accepting handouts. Or rather, we began allowing white Americans to create an illusion of progress. There is no greater example of this than the morally contemptible practice of affirmative action.

## THE NEGATIVE RESULTS OF AFFIRMATIVE ACTION

Of the myriad bad-faith systems put in place by our government to "help" blacks, there is none more verifiably useless, or more positively discriminatory, than the practice of affirmative action. Typically, media coverage of affirmative action in the educational system is focused on whether a qualified white or Asian college applicant is penalized in order to make room for an unqualified minority. What we do not hear about enough, however, is the inescapable truth that affirmative action harms the communities it was designed to help.

Economist and social theorist Thomas Sowell was an

assistant professor of economics at Cornell University in the late 1960s when he noticed that a significant portion of Cornell's black students were on academic probation. After investigating, Sowell determined that, while the university had taken drastic steps to eliminate racial disparities in its admissions process, it had also enrolled students who simply were not academically talented enough to be there. Indeed, those struggling students were not at Cornell on their own merit but because of affirmative action policies. They were given a seat for the sake of appearance and then were left floundering when they could not compete with their academically superior peers. In short, they were misplaced. Intrigued by the idea that a policy designed to help black students was actually hurting them, Sowell then did more research to confirm what he had observed at Cornell and found that the same held true everywhere: When you mismatch students based on the color of their skin, they do not perform well.

Affirmative action policies within American colleges and universities began taking shape in the early 1970s. Formally, they were inspired by President Johnson's Howard University speech, which was largely considered to have provided the framework for positive forms of discrimination. By 1965, Johnson had signed an executive order for positive discrimination in the workforce, requiring government contractors and subcontractors to take "affirmative action" by hiring minorities. It is fair to assume that the authors behind such policies had good intentions—but intentions are not results. Quite humorously, in the hope of amending their historical record of judging individuals based on the color of their skin, the academia put in place official policies and quotas, which worked by judging people by the color of their skin. Of course, on a more selfish note, these policies made white allies feel as though they were effectively dissociating themselves from the contemptible past of their ancestors. What better way to virtue-signal to those around you than to discriminate on behalf of a minority group, as opposed to against one? But as is true of all forms of discrimination, they eventually lead to regress.

Black students—just like all other students—will eventually be made to compete in the real world. Giving them early educational advantage solely because of their minority status—which is no different from *dis*advantaging them for the same discriminatory reason. In the end, it directly inhibits their ability to flourish, a notion which flies directly in the face of current progressive aims, which seek to give everyone a theoretical trophy to ensure that no one feels bad for losing. But that is a model based on feelings, not facts.

Factually speaking, masking inefficiency under an unde-served medal does nothing to edit one's true ranking. Rather, it creates an ecosystem of overconfident young adults, who will be crushed by the inevitability of the real-world markets, where there are no concessions made for the ill-prepared.

In the name of social goodness and feminism, I might decide to become a linebacker for a professional football team, and in the name of positive publicity, the NFL might decide to give me a shot. But the flowery intentions of nei-ther me nor the league would prevent my abysmal perfor-mance on game day. Similarly, when we falsely elevate black students to positions in which they do not belong it is the students themselves who are made to suffer when the figu-rative game begins. In theory, affirmative action is meant to level the playing field. In practice, it digs ditches.

I believe that the reason blacks continue to lag behind whites in terms of educational achievement is due to a cul-turally widespread belief that we should not be made to put in the same effort because of our earlier oppressive circum-stances.

Generations ago, black Americans understood that the only way to get ahead in life was through hard work. The idea of shortcuts and handouts through policy was not yet fashionable. And as Sowell noted, their willingness to work is the primary reason why the black community achieved what it did under far more harrowing circumstances:

> *The history of blacks in the United States has been virtually stood on its head by those advocating affirmative action. The empirical evidence is clear that most blacks got themselves out of poverty in the decades preceding the civil rights revolution of the 1960s and the beginning of affirmative action in the 1970s. Yet the political misrepresentation of what happened—by leaders and friends of blacks—has been so pervasive that this achievement has been completely submerged in the public consciousness. Instead of gaining the respect that other groups have gained by lifting themselves out of poverty, blacks are widely seen, by friends and critics alike, as owing their advancement to government beneficence. . . .*
>
> *Concern for the less fortunate is entirely different from imagining that we can do what we cannot do. Nor is the humbling admission of our inherent limitations as human beings a reason for failing to do the considerable number of things which can still be done*

*within those limitations. In America, at least, history has demonstrated dramatically that it can be done because it has already been done.*

Of course, the easiest way to determine that affirmative action is ineffective is to measure against the success that blacks have found in areas where it was not implemented. As an example, we tend to dominate sports. It's worth noting that LeBron James was never told that scoring one basket would equal four points for him because of his skin color. He was never told he was inferior or was brainwashed into athletic inferiority.

Black America also excels in music. On the top-ten list for the most Grammy awards ever won sit vocalists Stevie Wonder, Beyoncé, and rappers Jay-Z and Kanye West. None of them were given more votes because of the color of their skin. They were not graded on any curve. They simply created better music than their competitors and were rewarded for it.

It really is a shame that our education system refuses to apply the same method of hard work—the only method that has ever produced black greatness.

## PUBLIC SCHOOL TRAP

Before my family moved in with my grandparents, the only escape from my dysfunctional home life was school. From the first day of kindergarten, I looked forward to attending school each day not just to learn but to be in an environment that felt promising.

One of the first friends I made in kindergarten was a girl with blonde hair and blue eyes named Laura. We became fast friends, and she eventually invited me to her house for an after-school playdate. I had never been on a playdate before—at least not with someone outside of my extended family—and so I was unsure as to what to expect. What I encountered far exceeded anything within my imagination.

I still vividly recall the car journey to her house that day. I stared out the car window of her mother's oversized Suburban, startled, as the houses we drove past grew bigger and bigger. I remember being most impressed by the trees, regarding which there were just so many. There was so much forest, so much *life* outside of the existence of my family's small three-bedroom apartment on the other side of town. I was young then, and yet I remember feeling overwhelmed by the sense of it all; I had assumed that everyone lived like me.

Laura's home was a mansion in north Stamford, affixed

with an expansive playroom. *A room just for playing?* The concept defied my short-lived existence. I was an alien visiting another planet. Her bedroom was immaculate, and it was all hers—she didn't have to share it with two sisters like I did. She had a white Victorian bedroom set with porcelain dolls that neatly lined the shelves. Everything seemed so delicate. I was conscious of not wanting to break anything.

I often share this story when I give speeches today, because its lesson is important. The minds of children are but blank canvases, working in overdrive to process the world around them. How they process those experiences will steer their lives in one direction or another, toward their futures. Most important then is how adults answer their ever-blazing questions of "why." *Why is the sky blue? Why is the grass green? Why is Laura's house bigger than mine?* The immediate responses they receive, whether true or false, will begin to shape their relationship with society. In many cases, it can spell the difference between their ultimate success or failure in life. Like most children who spend the vast majority of their day in classrooms, I looked to my teachers and textbooks to provide a further understanding of the world, and because I attended a public school, those answers fit a clearly defined pattern: one that favored black victim propaganda over truth.

Parents would like to think that schools are safe environments for their children to grow up. Having come a long way since the days of Ruby Bridges, few can imagine that inferiority is learned in the classroom. But it is. Kids in schools all across this country are being taught the flawed concepts of white privilege and inherent black oppression, that their skin color makes them different. In public schools, children are taught that the difference between families like mine—those who live in low-income-housing buildings—and families like Laura's, is a matter of systemic injustice.

Over the slow years of our educational brainwashing, we are made to believe that slavery, Klan rallies, water hoses, and attack dogs during the civil rights movement are the prime explanation for every current ill that befalls black America today. This packaged theory is applied across the board: the poor are pitted against the wealthy, women are pitted against men, and so forth. This victim vs. oppressor method of teaching is particularly detrimental to the spirits of black youth. As it turns out, being told why we will not be held responsible for any of our shortcomings does little in the way of inspiring hard work.

Of course, the schools I went to never bothered to teach me anything that would lead to my concluding that perhaps

Laura's family was well-off due to her father's entrepreneurship. Perhaps it was his good life decisions that played a role in his business success. Nor would any of my lessons have explored the inverse culpability of my own parents' decisions; perhaps my mother's lack of a high school diploma and her decision to become pregnant as a teenager may have stifled her early potential. Perhaps my father's financial irresponsibility contributed to our economic instability. No, the school would not have dared teach a black person about the consequences of personal decision-making—not when the narrative of systemic oppression is so preferred.

And so, because instead of learning about free markets, capitalism, and entrepreneurship, today's curriculum overemphasizes the role that others play in our success. Students are being systematically disempowered, trained to resent the success of others.

And that creates a self-fulling prophecy of sorts. We can never attain what we resent, just as we will never achieve what we loathe. If money and success become the objects of our loathing and resentment, then we can be certain they will never be within our grasp. Our subconscious mind will reject its opportunity seeking to prevent us from becoming that which we have been conditioned to hate.

And beyond the tragedy of the education system's collective brainwashing of children against their potential is its outright failure to educate.

## REFUSING TO CHOOSE

In chapter 4, I highlighted how elementary-to-middle-school-aged black children are lagging behind their white counterparts in nearly every important statistical category. Unfortunately, the problem is only exacerbated at the high school level.

According to a 2019 report published by the standardized test company ACT Inc., only 32 percent of black 2019 high school graduates who took the ACT exam between their sophomore and senior years of high school showed college-readiness in the subject of English. And the data was much worse across other subjects of learning. Just 20 percent of black students met college readiness benchmarks in reading, and in the area of math and science, the percentages were 12 and 11, respectively.

This is troubling for the black community across the board, but black students who are considered "underserved"—that is, black children who like me come from low-income families and have parents who did not attend college—fare even more poorly:

✦ Just 9 percent of underserved learners who met all three underserved criteria met three or more ACT college readiness benchmarks.

✦ 21 percent of underserved ACT-tested 2019 high school graduates reported taking three years or fewer of math—more than double the percentage of non-underserved graduates (less than 10 percent) who reported this.

✦ Underserved students lag behind their peers in readiness for STEM (science, technology, engineering, and math) coursework. Consistent with the previous two years, in 2019 only 2 percent of students who met all three underserved criteria achieved the ACT STEM benchmark.

I needn't spell out what this data indicates for their futures. Without basic educational skill sets, their career prospects are lower, making them more susceptible to perpetuating the cycle of poverty that currently engulfs their communities.

It almost goes without saying that the public education system is largely at fault for these dismal statistics. Every day parents are handing their children over to dismal institutions that are clearly not best suited to prepare them for their futures.

But while black families have evidentiary proof that the public school system is failing their children, they remain convinced by the Left that it is their best, if only, option.

And though choosing the best school for our child should not be a politicized issue, it has certainly become one, as Democrats have convinced blacks that opting out of these institutions would spell catastrophe. Although numerous polls show that black Americans favor school choice (via vouchers that would allow parents to transfer the government funding already allocated for their children's education from a public school to a private school, charter school, or other institution of their choosing), left-wing politicians have nonsensically waged this option as an infringement on civil liberty. They make the extraordinary claim that the voucher system favors white families and is thus responsible for segregation in public schools. These are classic leftist misinformation campaigns, which control and constrain black progress.

It is unfathomable that black parents would continue to put their children's future at risk by pledging allegiance to abysmal public schools when the option to drastically improve their educational circumstances sits before them. It is even more unfathomable that liberals would ask them to. Is it not ironic that the same people who claim the American workforce is racist and that black Americans have a harder time securing jobs and moving up the corporate ladder would at the same time do all they can to prevent workplace preparedness by advocating against the best available paths for education? It is too often the case that those with the loudest voices against school choice are the very same Democrats who send their own kids to private schools. Their astounding hypocrisy is evidence of a more sinister intention, I believe. Perhaps Democrats simply understand that uneducated black children transform into uneducated adults, and uneducated adults are far more easily controlled by mass propaganda than those who think critically for themselves.

## ACADEMIA

There can hardly be a meaningful discussion about black people and education without discussing how black culture is one of the biggest contributors to black failure—because education is not deemed "cool" by many black students.

It is a sad fact that black students perform better academically when they are in a classroom of predominantly white students, as opposed to within predominantly black classrooms. The reason for this is never discussed, because it points to an internal problem which runs against the current code of black blamelessness.

The truth is that black Americans celebrate ignorance and accuse those among them who do not capitulate to Ebonics as "acting white." Nobody knows this better than me.

When I was in elementary school, students were not made to take standardized tests until we reached eight years of age, and even after the testing, we were not divided into classrooms based on the results. This meant that my classrooms were racially diverse. Accordingly, I was best friends with a young Hispanic girl and a young black girl simply because they were in my class.

When standardized testing began, I scored high enough that my third-grade teacher recommended I skip up to the fourth grade. As I had just switched schools and had just started making friends, I cried hysterically to my mother and begged her to let me stay in the grade I was in. She acquiesced, under the condition that I join an Extraordinary Learner's Program, which was a separate class that took place during the regular school day, for students who were considered high achievers. All of the students in this program, except for me, happened to be white.

Upon entering middle school, students were now placed

in all classes according to their standardized test scores. I was placed in a class group that had predominantly white students. I had two other black students in my class. Like all students, I made friendships with the people who were in my class. This meant the majority of my friends became white, a shift from elementary school days.

And that's when the bullying started.

The black girls who were in lower academic groups would block me in the hallway when I was trying to get to class and shout rude insults at me. One girl in particular would bump my shoulder every time I walked by her in a hallway. I chose to ignore them. In one particular instance, a black girl called me over to her table in the cafeteria to ask me a question. As I walked over, I knew it was a setup but felt I had no choice but to engage her. When I arrived at the table, she asked me plainly, "Candace, if I were to say to you 'Holla,' what would you say back?"

I answered her honestly. "I would say hello."

The entire table filled with black girls began wildly hollering with laughter, as I walked back to my table. Later, I would learn that the correct answer was "Holla back," a colloquial term popularized by the biggest hip-hop song of that time. Quite frankly, I wasn't much interested in keeping up with popular hip-hop songs, because J. K. Rowling had released another installment of Harry Potter—and I was racing home to read it every day, before any of my friends could spoil the ending.

All of this chalked up to their regular assessment that I was "acting white." And that was reason enough for black girls to try to humiliate me. Years later, I wound up sharing an art class with the girl who used to bump my shoulder. We became instant friends. I asked her why she used to bump my shoulder, and I will never forget the answer she gave me.

"I just thought you were stuck-up. I didn't realize you were cool."

She had convicted someone whom she had never even spoken to on the basis of little more than an assumption— an assumption based on the fact that I was in a higher academic group.

In high school, the girl who used to block me in the hallway and insult my outfits wound up in my geometry class. We too became fast friends. When I asked her why she used to pick on me, her answer was equally as absurd.

"I don't know. We just all thought you were a bitch," she quipped.

Of course, though convicted of the charge, I was never "acting white." My true crime lay in the fact that I was speaking proper English, correctly answering questions on tests, and reading books rather than keeping up hip-hop terminology. To my race, this represented some sort of a betrayal. I was not considered to be acting black. I was not conforming to an unwritten code of blackness.

Of course, the idea that black children who perform well in school are somehow "acting white" is in and of itself a racist assessment. It insinuates that intelligence is an attribute that belongs to white people. It signals to black youth that academic success is not for them. It fosters a culture where brighter black students must decide between wanting to be accepted by their race, or performing well in their studies.

The truth is that those who accuse others of acting white are themselves acting quite foolish.


## THE BURDEN OF FREEDOM

The fundamental issue is that after sixty years of Democrat allegiance, black America has been led to believe that we are exceptions to every rule. But we cannot be excused from hard work, studying, and good decision-making and then feign appalling surprise when we fail next to our peers. We cannot except ourselves from diligence and claim injustice over our varied results.

Holding us hostage in insufficient elementary, middle, and high schools is not enough. The education system, in tandem with the Left, grants us entitlements that do nothing but paint an illusion of accomplishment—an illusion that collapses at the first tremor of competition. And today's black culture—the residue of earlier racist misgivings about our capabilities, further alienates and limits our progress.

We so often hear the expression "freedom is not free," but what exactly does that mean? It means that freedom isn't a young woman in an open field with her head tilted toward the sun. It's more likely a young woman sitting at home, studying, even though she'd much rather be out with her friends. It's a young man, getting accepted into a highly ranked university on the basis of his outstanding academic performance. Freedom is personal responsibility. It's the sacrifices we make personally so that we may afford our lives certain privileges. Ronald Reagan famously said, "Freedom is never more than a generation away from extinction. We don't pass it to our children in the bloodstream. It must be fought for, protected, and handed on for them to do the same."

Though fought for, true black freedom was never achieved and protected. It's time for a new generation of blacks to take up the fight for it once again.

## 7

# ON MEDIA

Amy Robach's face was twisted in disgust, her voice thick with frustration. The words tumbled out of the ABC News anchor's mouth—one damning revelation after another, all caught on a hot mic. "I've had the story for three years," she said. "I've had this interview with Virginia Roberts. We would not put it on the air."

Robach was, of course, speaking about the damning evidence she had gathered about billionaire financier and suspected pedophile Jeffrey Epstein. And without knowing she was being recorded, Robach spoke candidly about the ways that she believed her employer, ABC, had stonewalled her story and opted to protect a potential criminal and his allies—instead of the young girls he had already harmed and those who could become victims in the future. Years later, after Epstein's arrest and the awakening of the general public to his monstrous behavior, Robach remarked that she was "freaking pissed" that she had been forced to keep quiet.

As the video of Robach began circulating on the internet, there were questions about who leaked the tape, what would happen now that the rants against her employer had gone viral, and how ABC planned to respond. But most pressing was this: Why would a mainstream media outlet like ABC, which claims to report the news, allegedly work to keep the news hidden?

What is most remarkable about Jeffrey Epstein's billion-dollar pedophilia ring is not the elaborate measures he took to recruit girls and whisk them off to his private island on his private jet—it is the men who accompanied him, including some of the Democrat Party's most prominent leaders. Among the high-profile names on Epstein's flight log: Larry Summers, secretary of the U.S. Treasury during the Clinton administration and director of the National Economic Council under Obama, and former president Bill Clinton. What is more, Clinton is shown to have taken at least twenty-six trips aboard the so-called Lolita Express.

According to Robach, she knew all of this. In her accidental testimony, she even declared that she had uncovered considerable dirt on the former president, but, again, she was prevented from revealing it on the air. She alleges that her superiors told her that "no one cared" about the Epstein scandal. If this is true, ABC is guilty of something far worse than simply prioritizing airtime; the network acted as a cover for its wealthy, liberal allies, guarding the immorality of some prominent members of the Democrat Party in order to maintain the allegiance of its millions of voters, including its 90 percent black voting margins.

We know this is not the first time an allegedly "unbiased" news organization has been revealed to be little more than a propaganda machine. In his book *Catch and Kill*, *New Yorker* columnist Ronan Farrow revealed that while working at NBC News, his bosses refused to air his early reporting on the sexual assault allegations against Harvey Weinstein. Farrow also alleged that NBC buried allegations of sexual assault and harassment that had been levied against former *Today* show anchor Matt Lauer. "In recent weeks, NBC has made a loud and clear statement about its values," wrote *Washington Post* media columnist Margaret Sullivan on November 5, 2019. "Profits matter more than journalism, ratings more than truth."

Sullivan is correct, and I'd offer that the state of our media is worse than she purports; for it is not just profits and ratings that liberal media organizations are after—it is control. By selecting what information is disseminated to the public and intentionally concealing what may expose competing narratives, media organizations directly influence public perception on a variety of topics, from foreign wars—to health care crises—and, of course, to race and politics.

Even as print journalists and TV anchors subvert the presumed impartialities of their industry, they continue to hurl reckless insults and allegations toward President Trump. The result is a propaganda-driven media landscape that works to intensify the black allegiance to the Democrat Party, by hiding the truth about its leaders and its motives.

## THE LIBERAL MEDIA'S LOVE AFFAIR WITH THE DEMOCRAT PARTY

There is perhaps no better starting point on the topic of biased media than the Trump presidency. Now that the mainstream, leftist media is united in their hatred for President Trump, there are virtually no lengths to which these outlets will not go in an attempt to smear his reputation, while carefully avoiding any actual reporting on his policies. That is because if the media focused only on Trump's policies (particularly as they relate to the black community), they would find little else to critique.

Here is one particularly amusing example: In late 2017 a media firestorm erupted among the usual left-wing news publications regarding the president's diet. The discussion began regarding the number of Diet Cokes he was drinking on a daily basis; soon the narrative was expanded to include his entire lifestyle.

On December 9, *Business Insider* published an article that dripped with latent aggression: "Trump drinks 12 cans of Diet Coke and watches 8 hours of TV per day." Three days later, the *Washington Post* followed up with their own story and the headline "Trump reportedly drinks 12 cans of Diet Coke each day. Is that healthy?" CNN, unable to pass up an easy attack on the president, resurrected the narrative a few months later with the story "A 12 Diet Cokes-a-day habit like Trump's is worth changing," which ran on March 9, 2018.

Later in 2018, nearly a year after the media first concerned itself with Trump's drink order, the angle of the story shifted once again. Reporters were no longer focusing their musings solely on the state of the president's health; suddenly Trump's affinity for Diet Coke was being presented as a problem for Coca-Cola and Diet Coke, as reporters speculated that the brands would be damaged by association with the leader of the free world. Case in point: the marketing trade publication AdAge.com ran the piece "Does Diet Coke Have a Trump Problem?" on September 25.

Currently, a cursory Google search of "Trump Diet Coke" will yield more than one million results—an overwhelming statement on the absurdity of the media's efforts to weaponize something as trivial as the president's beverage of choice. The liberal media had declared itself the moral authority, and Trump, with his penchant for Big Macs and Diet Coke, was deemed to have run afoul of this intimated high ground. Rather suspiciously, the parameters of morality that were so strictly applied to Trump's love of caramel-colored soda were somehow absent when Obama—who had a far more serious habit—was in the Oval Office.

The fact that former president Obama regularly smoked cigarettes while in office is widely regarded as one of the worst-kept secrets of DC insiders. During his second term in office, the occasional article addressed the issue: There was a debate about a photograph in which Obama is seen holding an object that looks eerily similar to a packet of cigarettes. Other pieces confirmed that he had, in fact, smoked as a college student. None of them, however, dared to vilify

Obama for his ongoing habit or his struggle to quit. If anything, the media exercised compassion and understanding for his desire to smoke, as though they were lending the flame to help him light up.

On June 11, 2015, *Time* published an article with the headline "Why It Matters if Obama Smokes (and Why It Doesn't)." In it, journalist Maya Rhodan wrote, "The general public doesn't care much [about his smoking]. A 2009 poll by CNN found that most Americans' views of the president aren't affected by his struggle to quit smoking and only a third wanted to see him give up cigarettes completely." After all, she stated, he had aced three physicals since taking office.

In her piece, Rhodan never went as far as asserting that Obama was, in fact, still smoking—even though all evidence seemed to point to the affirmative. What is more, she concluded her piece with a quote that suggested that his "potential" smoking habit "doesn't matter that much": "As a *Washington Post* writer noted, Obama has 'the best health care and the lousiest gig in the world,' so if he chooses to light up from time to time, he'll probably be just fine."

The contrast between the media's treatment of President Trump's less-than-stellar diet and President Obama's smoking habit could not be more stark. In Obama's years in office, the issue around smoking was casually ignored, swept under the carpet, or seen as little more than a minor blemish on the record of an otherwise brilliant leader. However, when Trump, a man who has never touched a drop of alcohol in his life, dares to drink Diet Coke (for which the medical evidence is nowhere near as damning as it is for smoking), the media declares his health to be a problem. My point here is not on either smoking or Diet Coke— I believe it is the right of every individual to make whatever life choices they want—but simply that, in a show of extreme bias and partiality, the mainstream media wildly shifted its philosophical standards from one president to the next, excusing the Democrat Obama before vilifying the Republican Trump for an arguably lesser sin.

This favoritism flies in the face of true journalistic principles, yet it is exactly what the modern media is known for. And it does not stop with this country's most recent commanders in chief, either. The media's overzealous defense of Democrats and the Democrat Party goes back much further, to one of the most racist men to ever occupy the Oval Office.

———

The mental gymnastics that have been performed by the modern media to both justify President Lyndon B. Johnson's racism while at the same time giving him credit for the successes of the civil rights movement of the 1960s never ceases to amaze me. Indeed, it is yet another great example of the preferential treatment that the modern arbiters of morality bestow upon their favored (read: Democrat) historical figures.

In reviewing the legacy of LBJ, most reporters focus on the passage of the Civil Rights Act of 1964 and the Voting Rights Act of 1965. These two pieces of legislation are lifted up as indisputable proof that Johnson was an advocate of the black community who was concerned about their welfare and ability to overcome generations of systemic oppression. However, there is scarcely any acknowledgment of the ways that Johnson directly sabotaged the black community.

Like FDR's New Deal, LBJ's Great Society initiative was designed to boost the economy, eradicate poverty, increase educational access, and otherwise restore America to its former greatness. And like FDR, LBJ sought to accomplish all of these measures by instituting unsustainable policies that failed to address the root causes of the issues at hand. Johnson lowered poverty rates in the black community, yes, but not by supporting black-owned businesses or addressing racist hiring practices and the racial income gap. Instead, he passed a series of bills that essentially distributed checks to struggling black families, thereby giving them the fish instead of showing them how to fish on their own.

In a 2018 article for *Politico Magazine*, Joshua Zeitz, who wrote *Building the Great Society: Inside Lyndon Johnson's White House*, inadvertently acknowledges the limitations of Johnson's antipoverty measures, stating, "The government normally measures poverty on the basis of pretax cash income, but when economists factor in noncash assistance including food stamps, Medicaid and housing subsidies (all products of the Great Society) and tax adjustments like the earned income tax credit (a product of the Nixon administration), the poverty rate fell by 26 percent between 1960 and 2010, with two-thirds of the decline occurring before 1980."

It is no surprise, then, that sixty years later, blacks, on the whole, are more dependent on those government handouts than ever. And this was, in fact, by design. For while Johnson's Voting Rights Act was instrumental in getting blacks to the polls in unprecedented numbers, particularly in the Jim Crow South, this turnout did little to leverage the black vote in ways that would be most beneficial for the community as a whole. Johnson's legislation essentially crystallized a long-term pact between blacks and the Democrat

Party that still exists today, lending credence to his alleged statement that he would "have those niggers voting Democrat for the next two hundred years." There is some uncertainty about whether Johnson actually made that bold claim, but even if he did not, a quote attributed to the president by numerous historians and publications lays bare the actual intention behind his historic civil rights legislation:

> *These Negroes, they're getting pretty uppity these days and that's a problem for us since they've got something now they never had before, the political pull to back up their uppityness. Now we've got to do something about this, we've got to give them a little something, just enough to quiet them down, not enough to make a difference. For if we don't move at all, then their allies will line up against us and there'll be no way of stopping them, we'll lose the filibuster and there'll be no way of putting a brake on all sorts of wild legislation. It'll be Reconstruction all over again.*

Indeed, LBJ would allege to save us from poverty and the night-riding Klansman; we would repay him, and the Democrat Party, with our blind allegiance for generations to come.

But we do not have to focus on LBJ's political maneuvers to know that he never had the best interests of blacks in mind and was, actually, a staunch racist. For evidentiary proof one need only look at how he treated the black people who were closest to him.

In his MSNBC article "Lyndon Johnson was a civil rights hero. But also a racist," Adam Serwer carefully outlines the myriad ways LBJ revealed his true feelings about blacks, often with prodigious use of the n-word. Serwer refers to the biography *Master of the Senate: The Years of Lyndon Johnson*, written by Robert Caro. In the book, Caro reveals that Johnson referred to civil rights legislation as "the nigger bill"; he also discusses an incident detailed in the memoir of Robert Parker, who worked as LBJ's chauffeur. Johnson had asked Parker if he would rather be called by his name as opposed to other, degrading titles, including "boy," "nigger," or "chief," but when Parker answered in the affirmative, Johnson balked. "As long as you are black, and you're gonna be black till the day you die, no one's gonna call you by your goddamn name," Johnson is said to have replied. "So no matter what you are called, nigger, you just let it roll off your back like water, and you'll make it. Just pretend you're a goddamn piece of furniture."

Remarkably, Serwer, like most other members of the mainstream media, sidesteps the obvious to push a more favorable leftist agenda. "Lyndon Johnson said the word 'nigger' a lot," Serwer wrote. But he was also, at least according to Serwer, "an uncompromising racial egalitarian whose idealism was matched only by his political ruthlessness." (Jack Bernhardt, writing for the *Guardian*, went as far as saying that Johnson, while "a truly awful man," was still his "political hero.")

Perhaps I missed something while I read Serwer's thousand-word ode to LBJ, but the usage of a derogatory slur plus a refusal to refer to one of his employees by his given name hardly make for an egalitarian perspective. We should not forget that before his presidency, while serving in Congress, the Texas-born Johnson almost always voted within the racist southern bloc, known as the "Solid South." These were the group of congressmen responsible for blocking any civil rights legislation that might begin to undo the centuries of oppression blacks faced in America.

But Serwer, truly adept at the aforementioned mental gymnastics, seemed to dismiss these indelible truths, noting simply that "Johnson was a man of his time, and bore those flaws as surely as he sought to lead the country past them." Ah, yes. It makes perfect sense that the president of the most powerful country in the world sought to lead the country before even leading himself.

LBJ's actions and record speak for themselves, absent the need for postmodern Dem-splaining. It is the historical record of racist voting, the racist language, the racist policies, and the allegiance to a racist party that were there for all to see, culminating in the greatest hoodwinking of the black community to ever take place. In one fell swoop, the welfare policies of 1960s Democrats laid waste to black families and homes, crushing aspirations and the entrepreneurial spirit that had once defined our community. The media, however, continues to treat LBJ as though he is one of the great totem poles of tolerance and virtue in the twentieth century, a shining beacon of civil rights in an age of bigotry. Meanwhile, Trump is cast as the avowed racist, even as the black unemployment rate hits new lows and which, before the mandatory lockdowns for Covid-19, stood at around 5.5 percent, down from the nearly 8 percent when he first took office.

LBJ and the racist history of the Democrat Party can help us understand how it is plausible that Joe Biden, a well-known and well-respected politician, managed to get away with citing Robert Byrd, a West Virginia senator who had previously held the position of Exalted Cyclops within the Ku Klux Klan, as his mentor.

With the help of the mainstream media, the Democrats have assumed the mantle of tolerance and liberalism, despite having had the most racist history of almost any major Western political party. The truth has been twisted to fit the preferred narrative of liberal news organizations so that those with whom they disagree are depicted as pantomime villains.

While the intentions of Lyndon B. Johnson have been called into question, those of the media are clear: ignore the truth, deal out virtue to those on whom their favor falls, and keep blacks shackled to the Democrat plantation.

## THE LIBERAL MEDIA'S CONTEMPT
## FOR THE BLACK COMMUNITY

If the media sought only to convince black Americans that Democrats were inherently blame-free and Republicans were incapable of virtue, that would be one thing, but their efforts do not stop with conservative witch hunts and a liberal hero complex. Instead, the media also makes clear its contempt for the black community through its reinforcing of the victim narrative, thereby perpetuating us back into the arms of our liberal saviors. There is no better illustration of this than media coverage of Black Lives Matter, an organization that conveniently received a multimillion-dollar injection from the notoriously liberal George Soros's Open Society Foundation.

The narrative that black men are routinely discriminated against and slaughtered by white police officers has become a dominant theme across mainstream media, inspiring protests, boycotts, and clashes with police officers. Across social media, footage of black men dying at the hands of white police officers has received hundreds of millions of views, garnering an emotional response from many who have decided that police brutality is a problem that needs to be solved. Of course, virtually no American would stand in support of something as horrific as police brutality, but the truth is, the issue of blacks being murdered at will by vigilante police officers is but a dishonest distortion, blown out of proportion by the liberal media's foundational need to highlight the suffering of the black community—whether real or imagined.

In an op-ed published by the *City Journal* on September 25, 2017, writer and attorney Heather Mac Donald used indisputable numbers to dispel the narrative that the killing of black men by white cops was such a frequent, senseless occurrence that all black mothers ought to keep their sons locked up in their rooms. While Mac Donald notes that the number of murdered black people increased by 900 from 2015 to 2016 (this, after a 900-victim increase from 2014 to 2015), she emphasized the point that white police officers are not responsible for those homicides. "Contrary to the Black Lives Matter narrative, the police have much more to fear from black males than black males have to fear from the police," Mac Donald wrote. "In 2015, a police officer was 18.5 times more likely to be killed by a black male than an unarmed black male was to be killed by a police officer."

What is more, Mac Donald suggested that a so-called Ferguson Effect may actually perpetuate more violence in black communities, as protests have emboldened criminals, inspiring defiance and disrespect, if not outright violence against men who are not paid nearly enough to police dangerous communities. And, in many cases, they are not anymore. Mac Donald noted that "[c]ops are backing off of proactive policing in high-crime minority neighborhoods," continuing, "Having been told incessantly by politicians, the media and Black Lives Matter activists that they are bigoted for getting out of their cars and questioning someone loitering on a known drug corner at 2 a.m., many officers are instead just driving by." The result? Many black communities are suffering from even more violence, which claims even more lives.

More current research also supports Mac Donald's perspective, shattering protestors' claims that she represents "white supremacist and fascist ideologies," as was reported by the *Washington Post* following the cancellation of a 2017 Mac Donald speech that was to be held at Claremont McKenna College.

The FBI's 2018 data on homicides clearly shows that blacks do not need to be protected from white police officers—they need to be protected from themselves. Of the 2,925 blacks who were killed in 2018, 2,600 of their murderers were other blacks; only 234 were white. I need not point out the fact that even if those 234 white-on-black homicides were all committed by cops (they *were not*), blacks are still 11 times more likely to be killed by someone within their own community. In fact, in 2016, at the height of Black Lives Matter protesting, black Americans had a higher chance of being struck by lightning than being shot unarmed by a police officer.

Additionally, new research from Michigan State University and the University of Maryland dispels the myth that killings of blacks by white police officers are somehow racially motivated and disproportionate to the number of white people killed by white cops. It finds, instead, that the most relevant data regarding police shootings is the amount of violent criminal behavior within the community—not race.

"Our data show that the rate of crime by each racial group correlates with the likelihood of citizens from that racial group being shot," said Joseph Cesario, a coauthor of the report and a professor of psychology at Michigan State University. "If you live in a county that has a lot of white people committing crimes, white people are more likely to be shot. If you live in a county that has a lot of black people committing crimes, black people are more likely to be shot. It is the best predictor we have of fatal police shootings." Even when black people are killed by police officers, Cesario noted that it is more likely to be at the hands of a black officer than a white one. "[T]his is because black officers are drawn from the same population that they police. So, the more black citizens there are in a community, the more black police officers there are."

For those who believe that cop killings are simply due to excessive force, Cesario's report contradicts that notion as well, revealing that between 90 and 95 percent of civilians who were killed by police officers were violently attacking either the cop or another person when they were killed. And while the media loves to report that blacks are repeatedly gunned down when their cell phone or another item is mistaken for a gun, these incidents are rare.

So the question is, if Mac Donald's perspective, Cesario's report, and the FBI's data are all true, what does the media gain by presenting an opposing, false narrative? Why would news organizations seek to frighten an entire community with tales of excessive, unprovoked violence? The answer is simple: by portraying blacks as sitting ducks or target dummies for trigger-happy cops, the entire black community is made to feel victimized and, thus, in need of a (Democrat) savior.

Suffice to say that when I present these facts in front of college campuses filled with Black Lives Matter supporters, I am regularly shouted down and booed.

---

I am constantly amazed by how much of the Democrat Party's platform is based on hypocrisy and the suspension of any rational thought. After all, while liberals are up in arms about the environment, using "science" as a justification for shoving statistics on global warming and rising sea levels in the face of every Republican they meet, they conveniently overlook the subject of "science" as it pertains to gender. It seems we can rely on the absoluteness of science when determining whether our planet will be habitable in one hundred years, but if a child is born a boy—with the chromosomes and reproductive organs to match—leftists claim biology becomes optional.

Indeed, the left-wing media has developed something of an obsession with trangender issues over the last few years, but what is alarming is how heavily these ideas are being forced upon the black community. While black families have only 9.5 percent of the median wealth of white families, three out of four black children are born to unmarried parents; and of the 36 percent of blacks aged 18 to 24 who are enrolled in college, only 42 percent will graduate (most of them black women), we are somehow being told to instead focus on murders of black trans women.

Of course, no innocent life should be taken prematurely, but if we are going to look at murders in the black community, should we not prioritize more significant areas, as in Chicago, where from January 1, 2018, to July 31, 2019, 687 black people were murdered, the equivalent of 38 murders *per month*?

But the media is not designed to empower the black

community with truth. Instead, it chooses to honor the twenty-two black trans women killed in 2019 with a newly minted "Transgender Day of Remembrance." Never mind that CNN pointed out that the twenty-two black trans women who had been killed represented the entirety of the murdered trans population, once again squarely positioning this matter as a black issue. And never mind that, as a whole, the black community is quite socially conservative. This is emblematic of how the Left views and speaks to the black community, pandering to nonexistent struggles while failing to address what matters the most.

The liberal media perceives black Americans as failures. They capitalize on our emotions with content that inspires more hate and more anger, rather than disseminating messages of empowerment. Ultimately, they are the ones empowered; the media is in control.

Whether it be pushing anti-Republican rhetoric (even as they protect their Democrat heroes) or convincing black America of its perpetual victimhood, the end result is still the same. The media is co-opting our right to think for ourselves and form logical, rational deductions about the world around us. At outlets like CNN, ABC, and NBC, reporters and anchors spoon-feed political and racial propaganda that limits our willingness to think, and act, critically. And it is all by design—the manifestation of LBJ's declaration that his efforts would have blacks voting Democrat for the next two hundred years.

It is comical that the Left brushes off Trump's accusations of "fake news" as antijournalist drivel when, in fact, it is their LameStream Media (to quote the president) that has been found guilty of suppressing the truth and obstructing countless journalists' reporting processes. Indeed, my other title for this chapter was going to be "On Hypocrisy."

## 8

# ON EXCUSES

I have spent a considerable amount of time trying to frame the personality types that fall for the verifiable nonsense of the Left. Who are the people that so quickly arrive at the illogical conclusion that America, which is held in the estimation of most as the greatest provider of opportunity in the world, is somehow wrought with irredeemable injustices? Who are the people that not only want, but *need* this narrative to be true?

In my experience, they tend to be people who regret their life choices and need to dissolve internal regret via some intangible, external force.

For the last ten years, I have been close friends with a young woman named Alexa. Alexa and I met interning one summer for a fashion magazine. She had come by the position with a bit of luck. She was waitressing in Brooklyn, trying to make ends meet as she pursued a career in acting, when one of the magazine editors sat down for dinner at one of her tables. The two of them got to talking, and a few weeks later, Alexa was working in a fashion closet. I had come by the position with a bit of persistence. I spent hours at a coffee shop every day for a week and applied to any and every internship opportunity related to journalism that I could find on the Web.

Alexa and I were natural allies. While most of the other interns were wealthy and connected, with family members who bankrolled their lifestyles, Alexa and I were two broke girls without any clue as to what we were doing, trying to make it in New York City. I envied Alexa's passion for the arts and her lust for life. I even envied the way she'd nonchalantly smoke cigarettes as we'd sit and chat over our coffee breaks. She seemed to me to be the freest person in the world, untethered by the pesky demands of life.

It did not come as a surprise to me, then, when just a few weeks into the internship, Alexa announced to me that she was going to quit the program. She was too tired, spread too thin, and saw no value in working at a corporation filled with unhappy women who were of no consequence to her life's ambitions. I remember admiring this act of defiant bravery and wishing that I possessed the same free-bird spirit within me.

The next few years felt like a blur. We remained good friends, living upon what felt like two diametrically opposed planes of reality. I spent my time counting every red cent that I had, desperately seeking any and every available net-working opportunity in Manhattan. Alexa spent time party-ing in Brooklyn, picking up acting gigs, and waiting for her big break. I was consumed with bringing my bank account out of the more than $100,000 debt that I had accrued via student loans. Alexa was consumed with acting classes, indie film producers, and putting together a meaningful reel that she could send around to casting directors.

Eventually, I landed a job in finance and finally began making enough money to pay down my loans, plus store a bit into savings. When Alexa and I would meet to catch up, her lectures to me were always the same; she didn't under-stand why I was living such a boring nine-to-six existence. She felt that I was choosing money over happiness. And though secretly still admiring her convictions, I cautioned her against not having more of a plan. We complained to and advised one another in a way that only two broke twenty-two-year-olds, fighting for a place in this world, could do. We had exactly nothing and everything in common.

Almost four years to the day that we met, Alexa called me quite frantically in need of a place to live. She was divorcing her husband, a boyfriend she had married on a whim, because she told me that he was a drug abuser. She didn't have the money to hire a lawyer and needed someone who could help her sort through the steps. I let her move in with me temporarily, meticulously working with her through all the paperwork, until everything was properly filed.

The entire experience brought Alexa to a reflective point. She was sensing that she needed more structure and was growing tired of trying to make it as an actress in Brooklyn.

By then, I had been promoted to a more senior position at the firm I had worked for, and we were by chance looking to hire assistants. I pleaded with Alexa to take the job. She would no longer have to live paycheck to paycheck, I argued. She could start a savings account. She would have excellent benefits and begin making meaningful network connections. And she didn't have to give up her beloved acting classes, either—she could simply convert them into a weekend hobby. I could sense a shift in her. I knew that she was at a crossroads and ready for the change. Alexa came in for an interview a few days later and met with our team. They loved her and I was given the clearance to formally offer her the position. I was ecstatic to deliver her the good news and she was overwhelmed to hear it. I only asked that she take the weekend to *really* consider the position, before committing to it. I didn't want to jeopardize my professional reputation by recommending someone who would quit a few months later—leaving us on the hook to find a replacement.

When the weekend ended, Alexa called me and told me her answer. She thanked me profusely, but she simply couldn't give up on her dream. She knew in her heart that she could make it as an actress and now, at the ripening age of twenty-six, she couldn't squander her last good years being trapped inside an office. Besides, she had a script she had been working on for a series. She was going to dedicate every waking moment of her time and energy into perfecting it. I remember feeling both slightly disappointed but overwhelmingly proud of her for not giving up her passions. I felt that familiar flutter of envy at the beautiful persistence of her dreams.

*Perhaps she was right. Perhaps I had committed to a boring life and become a slave to my responsibilities. What had hap-*

*pened to my childhood dream of becoming a writer, anyway?*
*Was I missing out on taking chances in my own life?*

Shortly thereafter, Alexa decided to leave Brooklyn for
Los Angeles. It was for her a spiritual calling and one that
she felt would at long last precipitate the creative successes
she was so deserving of. Meanwhile, I stuck to the now familiar beat of Wall Street, inching closer and closer to my
debt-free goal. In a world dictated by good intentions, I
would pause here to tell you that Alexa *did* make it in
Hollywood, simply because it was what she wanted most. In
the idyllic world painted by socialists, our desires ought to
be enough. Angelina Jolie (under government instruction,
of course) would be made to divvy up the acting roles she
earns among all other aspiring actresses, because that would
be fair. In a socialist reverie, we all deserve the same outcome. Our individual interests, talents, and choices become
meaningless. The same result would be guaranteed for all,
no matter how little or how much they put into it.

But the inexorable truth is that no such utopia can exist
because it runs counter to the human spirit. Free markets,
then, are a natural predicament.

Sometimes people learn this through tough experiences,
and Alexa learned it after spending a decade of her life trying to catch that big break.

As it turned out, she wasn't the only person trying to peddle a script in Los Angeles. As the tough reality of her choices began to manifest, Alexa became increasingly drawn to leftist mantras about the world. Today she tells me that she didn't make it in Hollywood, not because the odds to do so were implausible, but because of an inherent xenophobia that exists in the industry as a whole. It was because of her accent that she didn't land certain roles and because of a sexist environment that, as a proud feminist, she could no longer bear. As is true with so many leftists today, Alexa doesn't just want this dire version of America to be true, she needs it to be. Because if it isn't, she will be forced to accept the bitter reality of her own poor decision-making.

Alexa gave up stable opportunities in pursuit of the much-storied Hollywood dream, and after failing to make it in Los Angeles, she moved back to her native country.

My dear friend Alexa, once a daring, vivacious twenty-year-old young woman with a world of possibility before her, has now transformed into a thirty-two-year-old whom I struggle to connect with.

There is trace resentment in nearly every sentence she utters, a systemic struggle to which she can point to explain away her every shortcoming. Where once conversation flowed freely between the two of us, it is now mitigated by the trappings of political correctness. There is an unspoken understanding between two old friends to keep honesty dammed, lest it unnecessarily destroy our good friendship.

I share the story of Alexa because she is the avatar of so many leftists whom I come across today. They are as furiously committed to exposing the injustices of society as they are to never honestly assessing their own life choices.

*No, they aren't bitter at their own circumstances, they're just "woke" to the world's.*

Leftists need to believe that success is evil in order to digest their own failures. It becomes easier to say that Hollywood is somehow racist, xenophobic, or bigoted than it is to accept basic business realities like market oversaturation. There are millions upon millions of aspiring actresses, and only so many blockbuster hits and sitcoms to go around. My guess is that had Alexa dedicated those ten years to becoming a pediatric brain surgeon, she would not today be alleging discriminations.

## THE OTHER PATH

Contrast Alexa's story with a man whom I recently had the pleasure of interviewing, Dr. Ben Carson. In addition to being raised by an illiterate single mother, Carson grew up in Detroit in the 1960s. Needless to say, racial strife was widespread. Throughout elementary school and most of junior high, Carson attended predominantly white schools, where he became known as a "dummy." This was no doubt partially due to the racial climate, but his initial pitiful academic performance lent truth to the slander. Carson's mother, a divorcée working as a domestic in white homes and barely making ends meet, knew that her sons were not doing well in school. Mrs. Carson wanted a better life for Ben and his brother, and because she knew that education was the key ingredient to a brighter future, she chose to implement changes that would prioritize their intellectual development.

She began by limiting her sons' time in front of the television set, allowing them to watch only two or three programs per week. In the rest of their spare time, they were to read books they'd borrow from the library, and produce weekly book reports. To be clear, these reports were not to be submitted to their teachers at school—they were extra-curricular assignments within the Carson household.

It was not long before Carson's grades improved and he rose to the top of the class. Apropos of the time, a white teacher took note of Carson's remarkable turnaround and criticized the rest of the class for letting Carson—a black kid—outperform them. Carson would have had every right to feel angry or dejected by the racist shaming, but instead, he used the teacher's words to power his ambitions. On that day, he made the conscious decision that he would always excel in whatever he endeavored.

And excel he did.

Carson graduated third in his class before earning an undergraduate degree from Yale and attending medical school at the University of Michigan. He would go on to become a world-renowned pediatric neurosurgeon, and he earned so many accolades and awards that as a twelve-year-old, I was made in school to read his book, *Gifted Hands*— Carson's autobiography, which would go on to be made into a movie.

But it was a speech that he would give in 2013 at the National Prayer Breakfast meeting that thrust Carson into the political spotlight.

Standing in front of a few thousand attendees, Carson told the extraordinary story of his youth, of the tragedy and triumphs that created the man he is today. He credited his countless successes to his mother's persistence. For despite the tremendous adversity she had endured in her own life— despite having been born into extreme poverty as one of twenty-four children, marrying at thirteen, and battling severe depression while raising two sons as a single mother, with nothing more than a third-grade education level—Carson's mother impressed upon her children that they could be limited only by their own beliefs.

"[She] never made excuses, and she never accepted an excuse from us," Carson said. "And if we ever came up with an excuse, she always said, 'Do you have a brain?' And if the answer was yes, then she said you could have thought your way out of [any problem]. It doesn't matter what John or Susan or Mary or anybody else did or said."

In his life's retrospect, Carson remarked that it was his mother's constant encouragement to ignore the words and actions of others by taking full responsibility for themselves that was "the most important thing she did for my brother and myself." "Because if you don't accept excuses," he added, "pretty soon people stop giving them, and they start looking for solutions. And that is a critical issue when it comes to success."

Carson's mother continued to push her sons even as friends criticized her for keeping two young boys locked up in the house and reading books. "They're going to hate you," they warned. Initially, Carson did hate those extra assignments. He didn't want to spend his afternoons and evenings curled up with a book—that is, until he did:

*After a while, I actually began to enjoy reading those books because we were very poor, but between the covers of those books I could go anywhere, I could be anybody, I could do anything. I began to read about people of great accomplishment, and as I read those stories, I began to see a connecting thread. I began to see that the person who has the most to do with you and what happens to you in life is you. You make decisions. You decide how much energy you want to put behind that decision. And I came to understand that I had control of my own destiny.*

In considering Carson's story, I can't help but wonder, what if? What if the black community as a whole made the decision to let go of every excuse that we perceive to be holding us back? What if we taught ourselves to see only opportunity, rather than opposition? What would happen if we harnessed the power within us, to work harder and do better? What would America look like if we became the embodiment of our ancestors' dreams?

## SHAME: A FORCE FOR CHANGE

Every black tale of success—whether it be the life of Thurgood Marshall, Oprah Winfrey, Tyler Perry, or LeBron

James—carries the same critical wisdom: there is no substitute for hard work. Tyler Perry is a black man with no formal education beyond a GED, who earns hundreds of millions of dollars per a year. He both owns and operates a movie studio, which sits on a staggering 330 acres outside of Atlanta, a property that spans nearly three times the area of the famed Warner Bros. studios in Burbank, California. Perry accomplished all of this without any outside investment. Rather, his business achievements can be attributed to perseverance, a quality that is not dictated by race. Perry's acceptance speech at the 2019 BET Awards spoke directly to our community's need to stop making excuses and to, instead, take our futures into our own hands.

"While everybody was fighting for a seat at the table and talking about #OscarsSoWhite, #OscarsSoWhite . . . I said, 'Y'all go ahead and do that. But while you're fighting for a seat at the table, I'll be down in Atlanta building my own.'"

Lamenting the actions and behaviors of others does little to aid our success. Neither does removing ourselves from any personal responsibility. Today, it has become quite fashionable to dismiss ourselves from any shameful behaviors. We are taught to assume that any bad actions we take are the fault of larger, oppressive systems. When I speak to groups of young people across the country, this is the single behavior that I tell them to reject. Because shame, I believe, is a necessary emotion, one that helps us edit our future behaviors.

I often share the example of a college experience I had where, after drinking past the point of reason, I made the terrible decision to sleep with someone whom I would have never engaged in my sobriety. This took place before the era of #MeToo, before the media and education blurred the lines between regret and rape. I regretted my decision, and felt shame. Rather than portraying myself as a victim who was taken advantage of by a man who—just like me—had drunk past his point of rational decision-making, I allowed myself to sit with those feelings of shame and regret. I was twenty years old and fully aware that alcohol is a drug that takes us outside our usual character, and it would have been foolish for me to expect someone else to take better care of me than me. I was right to feel embarrassed. And because I fully accepted responsibility for my own actions, I was able to fully edit myself in the future. Most people today know that I rarely, if ever, drink alcohol (a decision I made years later, after I began hating the morning angst), and people who know me personally are likely to describe me as a straight-edge. My character today is thanks in large part to not just the mistakes I made, but the mistakes I owned, which allowed me to grow into a woman who I am proud to be.

But had I been born just a few years later, things may have been drastically different. I may have awoken nights after binge drinking and poor decision-making and headed into a police precinct. I may have told detectives that yes, despite the fact that I poisoned myself with a liquid that functions to lower our inhibitions, I was appalled that people didn't take me for the person I am in sobriety. And I would have become another victim of my own decision-making. Another oppressed woman in a patriarchal society, unwilling to accept any fault of her own.

It is unfortunate that with the all-too-fashionable claims of racism and sexism, people miss out on opportunities for growth. It is unfortunate that black America in particular is encouraged to deny that we play any role in our own misfortune, thereby forfeiting realistic means to transform.

## DEPTH IN DATA: THE HIDDEN STORY

My many detractors love to skew data points to present proof that systemic racism *really does* still exist in this country. While every person knows that, despite media portrayals, America is far from being a tyrannical country, leftists harp on statistics that, without proper context, lead some to believe that the odds are stacked against them.

Take the poverty line, for example. It is true that blacks are twice as likely to fall below the poverty line as whites (20.8 percent versus 10.1 percent, respectively, according to the United States Census Bureau's 2018 Income and Poverty in the United States report). But people fail to account for the fact that, across all races, single women (24.9 percent) and single men (12.7 percent) are far more likely to live in poverty than married couples (4.7 percent). Marriage rates have dropped dramatically in recent years, and (as we covered more extensively in chapter 2), the crisis of unwed mothers has had a dramatic effect on blacks. It's worth noting that only 6.9 percent of black married couples lived in poverty in 2006, while the poverty rate for nonmarried black families was a staggering 35.3 percent—a fivefold increase.

Similarly, we can lay waste to the concept of our oppression through incarceration, by simply correlating rates. It's an uncomfortable truth that black Americans commit a disproportionate number of crimes in this country. Of the 6,570 homicides committed in 2018, blacks were responsible for 2,600. We represent just 13 percent of the American population, yet we commit nearly 40 percent of murders. When I consider these numbers, I cannot feign surprise regarding our disproportionate presence within the criminal justice system. Surely, no one would make the argument that we should stop locking up murderers and drug dealers simply because they are black.

## NO PROBLEMS WITHOUT SOLUTIONS

Something that George W. Bush is well known for saying in his White House is the phrase "No problems without solutions," and this expression couldn't highlight a need in modern society better. Modern society has not only abandoned this mantra wholeheartedly but also added further caveats. Instead of "No problems without solutions," we have "problems with no solutions," and then "excuses for problems that have no solutions and no end"; finally, we have "excuses for problems that have no solutions and no end, but being given money by another group in society might make it better." The list of ways we can change this slogan gets ever longer and more specialized depending on which rabbit hole of leftist thought you fall into. My point here, and throughout this chapter, has really been to say that if we want to succeed in life, we must take the attitude of that original slogan—for every problem, we must tackle it with a solution. If that solution doesn't yet exist, then it is our job to create one; excuses will not fix the problem.

When we take that theme of victimhood versus victorhood, do we think the victors of this world returned home, glum and dejected, with excuses to their problems? Every great hero, ancient or modern, has fought against odds and overcome them; to their problems, they have found solutions. Of course, we do not need to define ourselves in such charismatic fashion; not all of us need be heroes or villains, but we are all challenged in our unique ways every day in life. It is in these small challenges that we are defined, because each of those small challenges builds to ultimately overcoming an even bigger challenge. And that is the harder path. No politician ever won an election with the slogan "be more responsible" or "don't make excuses for your failures."

My personal journey to success features no heroic feat: I got up every day and went to work. Boring, monotonous work. Work, however, that paid the bills, bit by bit, step by step, and helped me save and pay off my student loan. Dr. Carson was born with no superpowers—he just read books. Now he's the secretary of housing and urban development, a qualified surgeon, and a former presidential candidate. Tyler Perry's story? He skipped #OscarsSoWhite to focus on his own business. Excuses for failing to make tough decisions, failing to be honest with ourselves, failing to have responsibility will ultimately be the killer of dreams.

Black America has been fed excuses for generations. Every day excuses pollute the narrative surrounding our communities: police racism, generational slavery, wage gaps, etc. The list goes ever on and on, built around skewed data that helps support those narratives. Yet here I am—a girl who worked hard to pay off her loans, who had a few good ideas, started a YouTube channel, and is now being asked to speak around the country. Here I am, a girl from a small apartment and no financial means—who now knows the president of the United States. Why? Because I am the granddaughter of a man who got up at five o'clock in the morning to lay out tobacco to dry upon a sharecropping farm in the North Carolina, a man who worked so hard throughout his life that in his retirement, he purchased that sharecropping farm—a man who, despite growing up in the time of segregation, and despite surviving attacks from the Ku Klux Klan, never made any excuse. If my grandfather never made excuses, how could I? If our ancestors never complained, how can black Americans complain today?

# 9

## ON FAITH

I am always a bit amused to come across conservatives who claim they have no faith. I find myself wondering just what exactly it is they believe they are conserving. You need not be religious to know that Western civilization was built upon Judeo-Christian values. The principles of Western society are deeply aligned with the principles of the Bible. Quite naturally, any meaningful attempt to comprehend exactly what the Left is attempting to undo will bring you to the topic of faith.

Our humanity is defined by two basic desires: that of the material and that of the eternal spiritual. On the material side, we are obsessed with provisions of everyday life: money, charity, power, service, ambition, sacrifice. All these elements relate to our place in this world—and our desire to be perceived as influential, perhaps as selfless by giving away wealth and provision or heralded as a great leader by accumulating power.

Yet there is the other, deeper desire—that humanity has long grappled with: that of the eternal spirit. This is the power that has driven men and women to forgo all things secular by taking vows of chastity or silence, or to exile themselves to distant lands in the pursuit of evangelism. In its quest, others have even committed themselves to the belief of martyrdom through suicide. *That* is the intangible power of the spiritual. It is how the most basic of childhood questions—"Where did we come from?" "What is our purpose here?" "What happens when we die?"—can morph into transformative life decisions that stem from the soul.

All of these questions and their answers can be boiled down to a single word: faith.

Because whether you believe in everything or you believe in nothing, you believe in something.

Everybody has faith. Whether it is faith in a traditional religious belief system or faith in nothing, people commit themselves to an intangible idea. Every minute of our every day is determined by little acts of faith: faith in politicians to lead us, faith in doctors to prescribe medicines for us, faith in the media to report to us. In each circumstance, we deposit a little belief in someone or something. If our faith is honored, it transforms into trust. But if that trust starts to corrode, we necessarily place our faith in some other person or thing—new leadership or new ideology, which we hope will restore our faith.

Faith, then, has been at the heart of the black American story.

## AMAZING GRACE

The hymn "Amazing Grace" is well known to most as a staple favorite at Sunday church services. The harmonious melody carries words that reflect, in many ways, the parable of the Prodigal Son. Yet few know the story of John Newton, the man who wrote the hymn. Newton was a slave trader from Great Britain without any religious convictions. In 1748, just off the coast of Ireland, his ship became caught in a storm that he was certain would end his life. Desperate, he called out to God for mercy. Having survived, Newton believed that God had delivered him from his circumstances and he committed himself to Christianity. Six years later, he gave up slave trading altogether to pursue theological studies. Soon after being ordained into the Anglican priesthood, he began writing hymns, among them "Amazing Grace." What is remarkable is that the hymn found no immediate popularity in Britain. Rather, it gained steam decades later in the American South, during a Protestant religion revival. Soon the song became a Negro spiritual, sung on plantations by black slaves.

In the story of John Newton we find a deep irony: a former slaver writes what will become a song that gives the enslaved what is perhaps the only thing that gives them the strength to keep going. Faith.

*'Twas grace that taught my heart to fear,*
*and grace my fears released.*
*How precious did that grace appear,*
*the hour I first believed*

In these lyrics one can imagine how the everyday fear in the hearts and minds of slaves may have been silenced, even if just for a moment, by the thought of something bigger than themselves. At the thought of something beyond themselves. It was a faith and a trust that they somehow belonged. In a word, providence.

Consider this. On August 20, 1619, the first ship arrived at the colony of Virginia, carrying slaves who would be bought by English colonists. Almost four hundred years later to the day, in mid-August 2019, a young black woman would be readying herself for a big day in Virginia. Dressed in white lace, that woman would walk down an aisle toward her soon-to-be English husband, to the sound of a congregation singing:

*Amazing Grace, how sweet the sound*
*That saved a wretch like me*
*I once was lost, but now am found*
*Was blind but now I see*

The irony of my wedding day was not lost on me. The meaning of the lyrics, the electrical current carried through the tangled web of both black and white history, was not lost on me. Our guests, of all different races, joined in a chorus and delivered us all, even if just for a moment, to something bigger than ourselves. I realized that I was the living embodiment of all that my ancestors had sung for, all that my ancestors had perhaps hung on for. In a word, providence.

There are not many positive considerations on the topic

of American slavery, but the unshakable faith that was instilled in the black community is certainly one of them. It became something that even slaves could leave behind for their children, something that has given black America perhaps a richer faith narrative than any other group.

## THE PROMISED LAND

Dr. Martin Luther King Jr., himself an ordained pastor, also reflected on faith and paid homage to the Creator God in his "I have a dream" speech when he stated:

> *I have a dream that one day every valley shall be exalted . . . and the glory of the Lord shall be revealed, and all flesh shall see it together. . . . With this faith we will be able to transform the jangling discords of our nation into a beautiful symphony of brotherhood. With this faith we will be able to work together, to pray together, to struggle together, to go to jail together, to stand up for freedom together, knowing that we will be free one day—*

His appeal to faith and to the glory of the Lord was surely deliberate. He knew that faith made black heritage rich in a way that transcended the material segregationist world. Throughout this new era of black oppression, it was the one area in which black Americans had white Americans beat.

During a more recent conversation with my grandfather, I asked him why it was that his children, my father included, wound up leading lives so outside of the framework that he and my grandmother provided. My grandparents lived like puritans. They never swore, never drank alcohol, and never missed religious services. And while certainly not meant as a condemnation, I was interested in the fact that their offspring had all been through divorces, were less religious, and were plenty open to partying and celebration. Was it simply a desire to live as they hadn't been permitted to in their youth?

My grandfather shot back an answer that rather startled me.

"It was the hippies. They ruined everything."

The hippies. The 1960s movement that rejected the mainstream, conventional way of living. They would come to be remembered as the "dropouts of society" who followed the tenets of love, drugs, and rock and roll. My grandfather's answer was interesting because the late sixties also saw a shift in the attitude of black Americans. The pacifist culture of Dr. King became obsolete. A louder, more aggressive movement was beginning to take shape with the concept of "black power" at its core. Shelby Steele, in his book *White Guilt*, described the shifting sentiment:

> *For King's generation of leaders, racism was a barrier in the path to black freedom, and the goal was to remove it. But for this new generation of black leaders, racism existed within a context of white guilt. . . . By the mid-sixties, white guilt was eliciting an entirely new kind of black leadership, not selfless men like King . . . but smaller men, bargainers, bluffers, haranguers—not moralists but specialists—who could set up a trade with white guilt . . . racism suddenly became valuable to the people who had long suffered it.*

Steele, himself a part of the angry black youth at that time, goes on to detail their political meetings, where blacks would repeat Marxist phrases such as "raise your consciousness." It was this quiet Marxist entry into black America that, as he posits, became "a precursor to the now common argument that racism is systemic, structural, and institutional." It is interesting that he underscores Marxism as providing the basis for their beliefs, although he, like many others, was unaware of it at the time. The genealogy of this mentality is, in my opinion, the single most important truth for black Americans to know; our modern ideas of oppression were fathered by communism.

Karl Marx, the German philosopher and socialist revolutionary behind the Marxist doctrine, is the father of communism. Many people today attempt to draw differences between communism and socialism—there are none. Karl Marx was the socialist revolutionary (see: Bernie Sanders, Alexandria Ocasio-Cortez) who coauthored the infamous *Communist Manifesto*, a political treatise on how a society ought to implement socialism. Socialism is the theory, and communism its implementation. Similarly, free markets is the theory, capitalism its implementation. Any individual who believes in free markets will openly identify as a capitalist, but you would be hard-pressed to find a socialist who will admit they are a communist. That's because, as discussed in chapter 5, it is homicidal. Author Ayn Rand best asserts this when she writes, "There is no difference between communism and socialism, except in the means of achieving the same ultimate end: communism proposes to enslave men by force, socialism—by vote." In other words, when a free society first votes in communism, that is socialism. It is certainly strange that the faithful black community would have become mixed up in Marx's theories, especially since Marx famously described religion as the "sigh of the oppressed creature . . . the opium of the people." His belief that religion ought to be repressed inspired the murderous reigns of Russian leader Vladimir Lenin and Chinese leader Mao Zedong, who mandated statewide atheism. Within the Soviet Union, this meant that the government sponsored a program to convert people to atheism. Religious property was confiscated, and believers were harassed and publicly ridiculed. And yet, unwittingly, faithful black Americans in the mid-sixties would begin uttering the philosophies from the communist man who instigated these offenses.

Similarly, when Fidel Castro led a Marxist revolution in Cuba to become its dictator, he banned religious celebrations, shut down more than four hundred Catholic schools, confiscated religious property, and jailed and expelled Catholic priests before declaring Cuba an atheist state. After the socialists voted Castro into power—suicide—he reigned as a communist dictator until his death in 2016.

It is clear that those who wish to assume dictatorial control of a state use socialism as their conduit to power, but why is the removal of faith necessary? Why did Karl Marx and the communist leaders who came after him deem it essential to destroy the pillar of faith?

And why was this ideology brought to black America?

"Raise your consciousness," blacks were told, in an effort to recognize that racism and inequality are, in fact, everywhere. Karl Marx wanted his working-class followers to realize the totality of their oppression. He wanted them to universalize it and to view it as everlasting.

And that is exactly what black Americans started to do.

The brilliance of socialist doctrine is its understanding that full state control can arise from a working-class revolution. Smarter men, in the pursuit of power, recognized that a class of angry citizens could be manipulated to overthrow any government, and would likely elect the leader of their frustrations to assume full control in their revolution's wake. A good socialist leader must appeal to the emotions of the masses. He must justify their anger to the point of moblike riots for revolution.

And moblike riots are exactly what black Americans began to initiate.

The mid-sixties saw urban race riots all across the United States. Bloodshed, burning, and looting became commonplace. The result? Black economic depression for decades to come in cities that once flourished. It turns out chasing "racist" business owners out of the city yields unemployment and created the desolate, impoverished inner-city conditions that we see today.

What is noteworthy, however, is that these riots took place *after* black Americans had been given equal rights to white Americans—not before, when reasons for rioting would have been much more obvious.

In essence, black Americans were certainly not becoming more oppressed but were instead being transformed into pawns for smarter men in the pursuit of power.

## THE GOD OF GOVERNMENT

Today, we are seeing a rebirth of Marx's socialist agenda and with it, the routine mocking of those who practice faith. Fundamental to the Left's hatred of faith is the fact that Christianity preaches the doctrine of the Original Sin. Christians therefore know that humanity is not perfectible, because the Bible teaches that we are all "fallen" from Adam and Eve. Their original disobedience of God's word sets up the subsequent and continuing rebellious nature of mankind. It is for this reason that Jesus says to his disciples in Matthew 24, "See that no one leads you astray. For many will come in my name, saying 'I am the Christ,' and they will lead many astray. And you will hear of wars and rumors of wars. . . . For nation will rise against nation, and kingdom against kingdom, and there will be famines and earthquakes in various places. All these are but the beginning of the birth pains." It is a reminder to followers of Christ that until the coming of the eternal world, humanity will always be under the curse of sin.

Socialism, of course, cannot survive if this is the commonly held belief, because they teach that faith in government is the conduit to a perfect society. The quicker the spread of atheism, then, the quicker the spread of government as the solution to our every problem.

Black America outstrips the rest of the United States when it comes to faith, still. According to a Pew study ("U.S. Religious Landscape Study," 2014), black Americans are both far more convinced of their faith and take their faith in God more seriously than both white and Hispanic America. In a stark contrast, black Americans say they believe in God with absolute certainty by a margin of 24 percent versus Hispanics and 22 percent versus whites. This is perhaps the reason that in America we have, rather unusually, a church that is named after a particular racial group. The "black church," as it is known, is an alien concept to most other societies. While there are certainly churches that cater to particularly ethnic or linguistic groups, it is out of the deep spiritual heritage that emerged from the Civil War and the era of segregation that black churches were born and continue to this day, well into the era beyond civil rights and racial inequality.

Yet, undeniably, the Left is gaining some territory. If we look at the trend of Christian faith, there are a few stark warning signs that the Left's mission is having some success:

In a 2019 Gallup poll, 25 percent of participants, when asked "How important is religion in your own life?," answered "not important," up from 12 percent in 2000. In the same poll, the number of those who say they have no faith has almost tripled, and those professing specific Christian faith have dropped from 82 percent to 67 percent. Separately, in a Pew Research study, church attendance on a monthly basis is being replaced by a few times a year or less. People who answered "yes" to church attendance monthly or more went from 54 percent in 2007 to 45 percent in 2019, while those who attended simply a few times a year had the exact opposite number trend over that same twelve-year time frame.

When it comes to the black church, the same theme is

observable. Again, Pew Research conducted a study that showed that between 2007 and 2014, black Americans' attendance at church dropped from 53 percent to 47 percent in the "at least once a week" category, while simple "belief in God" dropped from 88 percent to 83 percent. These numbers are not staggering drops, but over a seven-year period they do betray a continuation of the same theme: God is on the decline in America.

These points drive home a hard truth for all of America, both black and white: we are losing the base of our Christian value system. In the space of less than twenty years the Christian fabric that has underpinned our Western civilization for centuries has been picked apart at the seams by faithlessness.

As I suggested earlier, people do not simply lose faith—they replace it. The Left is trying to replace and transform faith. And they wish to separate black Americans from their faith in God in an effort to replace it with a faith in government and the Left's pursuit of "moral goodness." It is a model that espouses altruism and the inherent goodness of all involved, and includes no room for the truth regarding our fallibility.

Perhaps most revealing is the study of religious trends.

In a Gallup poll conducted between 1998 and 2000 versus 2016–18, one of the fastest subgroups to leave church was determined to be those who held a Democrat Party ID. In 1998–2000, 71 percent of Democrats attended church, compared with only a 48 percent attendance record in 2016–18, a drop of 23 percent, which was greater than any other age, education, marital status, gender, or regional subgroup.

As America pushes forward into the twenty-first century, the threat to faith within our national community has never been greater. The growing trend of secularization threatens the very documents that gave our country birth.

In 2019, at the San Francisco meeting of the Democratic National Committee, the Democrats adopted a resolution (unanimously) that stated the following:

*WHEREAS, religiously unaffiliated Americans overwhelmingly share the Democratic Party's values, with 70% voting for Democrats in 2018, 80% supporting same-sex marriage, and 61% saying immigrants make American society stronger; and*

*WHEREAS, the religiously unaffiliated demographic represents the largest religious group within the Democratic Party, growing from 19% in 2007 to one in three today; and*

*WHEREAS, the nonreligious have often been subjected to unfair bias and exclusion in American society, particularly in the areas of politics and policymaking where assumptions of religiosity have long predominated . . .*

The resolution goes on to state that the DNC recognizes "[t]hat religiously unaffiliated Americans are a group that, as much as any other, advocates for rational public policy based on sound science and universal humanistic values and should be represented, included, and heard by the Party."

There are two things that immediately jump out at me from the above resolution. The first is that increasingly the Democrats align themselves with the secular, and the second is that they are pushing for "universal humanistic values." On the first, it is alarming that one of the two major political parties of this country, which was built upon the truths of God and whose founding document states that God has endowed humanity with "certain unalienable Rights" as well as lauding Him as "the Supreme Judge of the world," should choose to both commend and move increasingly to embrace secular trends that are not in keeping with the original founding of the nation. Second, and arguably more alarming, is that they wish to transfer "universal humanistic values" into the moral conversation, but the age-old question of relativism then simply creeps back in: Who decides what these humanistic values are? The problem that all societies have found is that in seeking to replace eternal theological values, they can replace them only with material values that change over time. Thus begins the argument, why shouldn't the Constitution be changed every generation so that it can be updated to reflect the latest version of morality? We have already seen, in discussing the media, that the moral values of each generation change—imagine what this would mean for Americans if we removed the God-given values and aspirations that our Founders built into the documents that gave birth to this land?

The continued assault on faith by the Left was also evident when the words "So help me God" were removed from many of the swearing-in ceremonies of Democrat-controlled congressional committees in the aftermath of the 2018 midterms. Steve Cohen, a long-standing Democrat congressman from Tennessee, was quoted in the *New York Times* as saying, "I think God belongs in religious institutions: in temple, in church, in cathedral, in mosque—but not in Congress" and "God doesn't want to be used," the latter comment obviously betraying the direct line that Cohen has to the Almighty.

Small changes such as these are just the beginning of the walk to secularism that will eventually lead to a radical full-scale disposal of God within our society. It is no longer politically expedient for the Left to seek God, so they don't; look at any socialist society, as mentioned in earlier chapters, and you will see that atheism is the name of the game.

## JUDGMENT DAY

So where does this leave the conversation on faith? Well, quite simply, the Left wishes to drive a wedge between people and God in the same way that it has successfully driven a wedge between individuals and family. The Left understands that in order to grow government to a state of omnipotence, there must be nowhere else that its citizens place value and faith.

I have mentioned many times over that we cannot perfect humanity, but it is here, in a discussion about faith, that my earlier assertions find their true context. Because underpinning most of what drives the liberal agenda in America is the fundamental belief that there is a greater ideology than "all men are created equal," and that is the leftist belief that "all men are perfectible." They are driven, not just in America—but also further abroad, by this dishonest and impossible promise to the people.

And paradoxically, in their mission to destroy faith, they demand the same. They want faith in *their* vision, *their* principles, *their* ideals. Ultimately it is a vision born of arrogant pride. What the Left holds above all else is faith in themselves. Astoundingly, it is a desire to elevate the mind of man into the position of God. However, the expression "don't play God" is popular for a reason. Because doing so never works.

The Bible talks extensively about the pride of man, often citing it as one of the greatest sins against God. The Left's unholy alliance with godlessness and their desire for secularism will undoubtedly bring about disaster. Proud societies, arrogant societies, societies with a belief in the things of this world and without a belief in God, are those marked by God's wrath.

"For the LORD of hosts has a day against all that is proud and lofty, against all that is lifted up—and it shall be brought low" (Isaiah 2:12).

"Proud societies will be marked with strife: 'Where there is strife, there is pride'" (Proverbs 13:10).

I believe that at the very core of the national debate surrounding the future of our country lies the question of faith. And I believe most of the determination will be set by black America, and whether we remain steadfast to the only beliefs that have seen us through the many hardships we have faced.

Paul writes in the Letter to the Galatians that it is "for freedom that Christ has set us free . . . do not let yourselves be burdened again by a yoke of slavery." How prudent these words are for black Americans as we are being encouraged to replace God with government. The great biblical narrative of a fallen mankind and Christ redeeming that fallen state finds unique homage within the black community. First, we had slavery; second, we had the era of Jim Crow; and now, third time unlucky, we have Democrats entrancing us to their gods of welfare, poverty, and despair. We have found ourselves, yet again, in need of salvation.

Black America, much like the Jews in the Old Testament, has been liberated, but led somehow back into the wilderness by the false prophets of the Democrat Party.

There is much discussion in the Bible regarding false prophets and hypocrites. In the Book of Lamentations (2:14), commonly ascribed to the prophet Jeremiah, he writes, "Your prophets have seen for you false and deceptive visions; they have not exposed your iniquity to restore your fortunes, but have seen for you oracles that are false and misleading." What greater description could be penned of many of the leaders of the black community to this day?

The vision of black America that has been provided by leaders such as Al Sharpton and Jesse Jackson (both ministers) seeks to deceive, not restore the fortunes of our community.

In Matthew 7:15, Jesus warns us to "[b]eware of false prophets, who come to you in sheep's clothing but inwardly are ravenous wolves." These are the race-baiting hustlers who saw an opportunity after Dr. King's dream was realized. They are those who today stir up racial hatred and resentment for their own vanity and achievement; the very men who are supposed to lead the great saving of black America and who have been given the opportunity to do real good among our people have instead used the opportunity to further their own selfish ambitions. But indeed, it is for the scribes and Pharisees, the equivalent ancient leaders of the Hebrew community, that Jesus reserves his harshest words for:

> *Woe to you, scribes and Pharisees, hypocrites! . . . For you clean the outside of the cup and the plate, but inside they are full of greed and self-indulgence. You blind Pharisee! . . . For you are like whitewashed tombs, which outwardly appear beautiful, but within are full of dead people's bones and all uncleanliness. So you also outwardly appear righteous to others, but within you*

*are full of hypocrisy and lawlessness. . . . You serpents,*
*you brood of vipers, how are you to escape being sen-*
*tenced to hell? Therefore I send you prophets and wise*
*men and scribes, some of whom you will kill and cru-*
*cify, and some you will flog in your synagogues and*
*persecute from town to town. (Matthew 23: 23–34)*

It feels good to be reminded that the harshest of judg-
ments will be reserved for false leaders who signal virtue
but live opposingly. For those who preoccupy themselves
with preaching perfection because it fills them with
self-righteousness and self-importance, their day will come.
Today we see so many of these people: millionaires preaching against wealth, those who fly privately while lecturing
about the environment, those with armed guards, demanding we give up our guns. Hypocrisy is the game of the Left.

The story of black America is a long narrative of faith.
Even in our darkest moments of history, our hope was always
invested in the world to come. Much like the Hebrew slaves
in Egypt, we have been on a great journey of redemption. We
must put faith back at the heart of America, both black and
white. Saving America means rescuing the Judeo-Christian
principles that defined her. The increasing drift of secularism
within our nation holds dangerous precedent for moral codes

and values to be rewritten in the image of man, rather than that of God.

More than ever, we must remember the words of MLK:

*I just want to do God's will. And He's allowed me to go up to the mountain. And I've looked over. And I've seen the promised land. I may not get there with you. But I want you to know tonight, that we, as a people, will get to the promised land. And I'm happy, tonight. I'm not worried about anything. I'm not fearing any man. Mine eyes have seen the glory of the coming of the Lord.*

It is once again time to have faith.

# 10

# ON CULTURE

I t is difficult to imagine my grandfather, who exclusively wears khakis and a collar every day—feeling anything but mystified by the popular trends of black America today.

The Chinese philosopher Confucius, who lived between 551 and 479 B.C, wrote, "If one should desire to know whether a kingdom is well governed, if its morals are good or bad, the quality of its music will furnish the answer."

The music of my grandfather's young adulthood was largely imprinted by Motown Records, a black-owned record label with a score of soulful vocalists who sang predominantly about topics of love and family. His favorite group was the Temptations, composed of five black men out of Detroit, who always wore suits when they performed. Growing up, my grandfather and all eight of his brothers would perform dance routines to their many songs at our family reunions. During the famed annual "Owens Talent Show," the Owens brothers would line up across the stage and show off their coordinated moves to classics like "Just My Imagination" or "My Girl"—a favorite song of mine to this day:

*I've got sunshine on a cloudy day*
*And when it's cold outside, I've got the month of May*

Such lyrics remind me of a black community, spirit, and culture that I never truly knew but am deeply nostalgic for: my grandfather's black America.

If what Confucius speculated about music was true, then there can be no wonder about the state of black affairs today. At the time of writing, the number one song on the hip-hop billboard charts is called "Savage," performed by an artist named Meghan Thee Stallion and Beyoncé.

Here is the opening:

*I'm that bitch (yeah)Been that bitch, still that bitch*

Is it reasonable to assume that the black community which thrust the Temptations to the top of billboard charts, holds the same values and beliefs as the ones who today boosted Meghan Thee Stallion to the number one spot? Of course not. The truth is that in just a few short decades, black culture hasn't just transformed, but devolved.

Our culture today is much about achieving a status of "coolness" through the slow decay of morality: less clothing, more profanity, less education. We are fundamentally anti-establishment, and anti-conformity. An artist would be hard-pressed to land a number one track singing about family and love. Those days of black America are long gone.

The Democrats, of course, know this, and view black culture as their preferred means to garner votes around election time. Their candidates follow the belief that if they "act black," meaning, speak in broken English and regurgitate popular black phrases—it will be enough to earn respect (and votes!) from the black community. And in most instances, they have been proven correct.

A cringe-inducing scenario played out in 2016 when then–presidential candidate Hillary Clinton stopped by the number one hip-hop radio show, the *Breakfast Club*. Her objective there was painfully obvious: *Make these black people believe I'm cool, so they'll vote for me.* It is important to note that at the time of her visit, Beyoncé had released a wildly popular song, titled "Formation," in which the singer utters the phrase "I have hot sauce in my bag, swag"!

Certain to have been brought up to speed on this by her many staffers before she went into the interview, Clinton proved too eager to display her cultural hipness. When asked by the show hosts to name one item that she always keeps with her in her purse, the Democrat nominee perked up and without missing a beat blurted, "hot sauce!"

The hosts laughed nervously, apparently caught off guard by such a purposed response to a softball question. One of the hosts then clarified to her, "I just want you to know that people are going to see this and say 'Okay, she's pandering to black people again.'" It was a perfect opportunity for Clinton to say she was joking and to answer the question in earnest. Instead, she asked the host, "Is it working?"

It was a shameless moment that drew back the curtain on the lowly perception of blacks held by left-wing politicians. In retrospect, the exchange offered a preview of how Hillary would continue her campaign for the black vote; she never discussed policy. She never discussed how she intended to improve inner cities. She did however—just four days before Americans headed to the polls on November 8—opt to have Beyoncé and Jay-Z perform at her campaign rally. She had dutifully received the support of black cultural icons, and in exchange, she fully expected black Americans to hand in their votes.

And four years later in 2020, Democrat presidential candidate Joe Biden would pick up where she left off.

In a satellite interview for the same hip-hop radio show, Joe Biden spoke with the nationally syndicated talk-radio host and two-time *New York Times* bestselling author Charlamagne tha God. Charlamagne is a deeply respected leader in the black community who has proven unafraid to ask Democrat contenders tough questions. After a rather contentious fifteen minutes in which Biden did not let Charlamagne ask many questions, Biden announced that he had run out of time. Charlamagne told the presidential hopeful that he still had more questions, and asked that the candidate commit to a longer, in-person interview in the future.

In response, Joe Biden looked into the camera and declared, " 'If you have a problem figuring out whether you're for me or Trump, then you ain't black."

*You ain't black.* Just like that.

Rarely had any Democrat hopeful been so honest. While it has been abundantly clear to most conservatives that the Democrats do not believe blacks need to have their political questions answered—no one had ever risked communicating that sentiment so plainly—at least not publicly.

Biden's declaration clarified that for black Americans voting Democrat has come to be viewed not only as an expectation but as a condition of blackness. Left-wing candidates feel so certain that there is no variety of thought or experience among blacks that they are comfortable publicly stripping us of our identity, should we offer any objection to the status quo.

It is likely that Charlamagne had a few questions pertaining to Biden's problematic record on racial justice while he served in the Senate, particularly surrounding the topic of desegregation. In fact, Biden was so against the concept of mandating school integration that he once referred to the idea as "the most racist concept you can come up with," and, even up until a 2007 memoir, argued that the concept was "a liberal train wreck." Senator Biden also argued that it was *better* for blacks to be segregated, because we preferred it that way.

Perhaps most flagrantly, Biden was also a leading crusader and coauthor of the notorious 1994 crime bill, championing harsher sentencing policies that led to defendants' serving longer prison terms, which disproportionately affected black men.

And yet here he appears, years later in 2020, unwilling to answer any questions about his past misgivings. Because why on earth would black Americans need anything more than a basic instruction to vote Democrat?

Most troubling for me was Biden's usage of the word "ain't" during the interview. I've scoured the internet looking for clips of him saying "ain't" while speaking to a white person, and come up dry. It seems he reserves his broken English just as Hillary Clinton reserves her hot sauce: for the black community only.

But what do these incursions amount to? Should we be upset with Biden and Clinton for an apparent lack of respect? I think the better question is, Do we conduct ourselves in a manner that commands respect?

I believe wholeheartedly that Democrat politicians believe that black people are stupid. I believe they look at our culture of disrespect which was fostered not by a natural black identity but by the long-term success of Democrat policies; polices that debased our men, our women, and thus our families; policies that corroded the world around us and which we then transformed into our music.

I often hear from black liberals, "Candace doesn't represent the black community," and to that I always think, "and neither do you." No black American who participates in the modern culture of debauchery is representative of the glory of our ancestors. It has never been my goal to be viewed as a spokesperson for debasement. In fact, it is my unequivocal intention to be seen as an adversary to it.

I believe what the Democrats see in black America is an undereducated community of people who are overinvested in culture. Their methodology, then, is to maintain control of the culture as a means to regulate the black vote. It is well known that it is career suicide for any person in Hollywood to be explicitly conservative. If they share any perspective that pivots away from liberal orthodoxy, they are accused of racism and branded a Nazi. If they are black, they are accused of insanity. The left therefore employs culture—singers, actresses, and rappers—to brainwash black Americans into believing that they must think and vote as a monolith.

And what of these celebrities? The bible cautions repeatedly against the sin of idolatry:

"Little children keep yourselves from idols."

"Do not turn to idols or make for yourselves any gods of cast metal."

"The sorrows of those who run after another god shall multiply."

I used to have a lot of idols. I now have none. I have watched the black community be lured time and time again by "idols" into self-destructive behaviors. That, in my opinion, is the evil of Hollywood. It is Taylor Swift's, Beyoncé's, and scores of other chart-toppers' belief that their mere presence yields such divinity that they may command legions of fans to vote, think, and act according to their whims. Black culture has become rotted by such idolatry, the reins of which are controlled by Democrats.

Take the recent death of George Floyd, a black man who was killed by a police officer during a botched arrest in Minnesota. During the four years leading up to this incident, and because of the media's obsession with police brutality during the 2016 election cycle, I forewarned the black community that at some point in 2020 we could expect the killing of a black man to be widely publicized and immediately politicized. But when the video of George Floyd dying as a police officer pressed a knee into his neck hit the internet—not even I could have predicted the worldwide response.

It is important to note that as of this writing and now weeks into the nightmare that has swept America since this killing, we still have not seen full footage of what happened on that day. What we do know is that on May 25, 2020, police officers were called to the scene after a store clerk reported that a man had attempted to use a counterfeit bill. The caller described the man as being under the influence.

"He's sitting on his car 'cause he is awfully drunk and he's not in control of himself," the caller stated.

The phone-recorded video of the arrest made available to the internet shows George Floyd being restrained by a police officer's knee to his neck. Several times, Floyd says to the police officer, "I can't breathe." Five minutes into the video, Floyd appears to be completely unconscious. Minutes later he is transported into an ambulance, and we learn that he is pronounced dead some time beyond that.

There was an immediate national consensus that the officer in question, Derek Chauvin, was in the wrong. In a rare moment of political accord, pundits and leaders from both sides of the aisle demanded the officer's immediate arrest. After a brief internal investigation into the matter, Derek Chauvin was arrested four days later on May 29, charged with third-degree murder and second-degree murder. It was, by any reasonable estimation, extremely swift, agreed-upon action.

But nothing is reasonable in an election year.

Activist groups Black Lives Matter and Antifa immediately readied their engines. Within days, Minneapolis (the city where the incident had taken place) was on fire. Rioters burned and looted businesses and stores, as wider calls were made to carry similar riots out across the nation.

Celebrities came out in instant support of the protesters, pledging funds to bail out any person who was arrested. Los Angeles, D.C, Minneapolis, Atlanta, New York—all major Democrat-controlled cities—burned. Black business owners pleaded with the rioters to stop the madness, as they were forced to watch all they worked for reduced to ashes overnight. The rioters burned American flags; they burned police officers. Two lawyers, one a Princeton-educated corporate attorney, the other a Fordham University law graduate, were arrested for throwing a Molotov cocktail into a police patrol car in New York City. Police officers were ruthlessly attacked all across the country.

At the time of writing, fourteen black Americans have been killed in these riots. The rapid rate of death and destruction in black neighborhoods was of no apparent consequence to the protesters. Beautiful tributes to George Floyd poured in from all around the world. Joe Biden prerecorded a speech for his funeral. Murals were painted of Floyd all across the country, and journalists rushed to eulogize him as a "gentle giant." Celebrities, musicians, and politicians gathered in front of George Floyd's golden casket as the ever-nefarious Reverend Al Sharpton gave an empowered tribute, complete with several shots at President Trump, who was now somehow to be blamed for the incident.

"George Floyd's story has been the story of black folks. Because ever since 401 years ago, the reason we could never be who we wanted and dreamed to be is because you kept your knee on our neck," Sharpton bellowed. "What happened to Floyd happens every day in this country. . . . It's time for us to stand up in George's name and say 'Get your knees off our necks.'"

A series of televised memorials, in three different cities over the course of six days, were planned as a follow-up. Millions of dollars poured in to support the Floyd family. In a matter of days, George Floyd had been transformed into a martyr for black America, an iconic symbol of our inherent oppressions in a racist society.

Any individuals who did not post a tribute to George Floyd and Black Lives Matter were immediately branded racists. Culture had dictated that this was the corrective course of action, and any person who refused the mandate was publicly lambasted.

I kept quiet for more than a week—an eternity, in social media terms. I watched the all-too-predictable lie so carefully being woven, every fiber supported by Hollywood idols. I ignored many requests for me to comment on the situation, preferring to remain quiet and let Floyd's family grieve until I could no longer stay silent.

It was the death of David Dorn that was the final straw. David Dorn, a 77-year-old black man and retired St. Louis police captain, had responded to an alarm at a pawn shop that he was providing security for during the riots. Aware of lootings taking place, Dorn went down to defend the shop, and was subsequently shot and killed by a 24-year-old black man who was in the middle of robbing the place. His death was captured on video. I watched an innocent black elderly man bleed out onto a concrete surface, because "culture" had sounded the alarm on racism. No celebrities or Democrat politicians said anything about his death at all. No Floyd-level tributes were posted in his honor, or organized protests staged in his name. Because David Dorn had made the same mistake that 94 percent of black homicide victims make: he was killed by another black person.

Since it doesn't fit the preferred racial narrative, all of these much-more common deaths are ignored. Instead, attention is given to a circumstance that happens rarely—the killing of an unarmed black man by a police officer. Rarely, as in, a black person is more likely to be struck by lightning than to die unarmed at the hands of police. Rarely, as in, during the year 2019, out of an approximate 10 million arrests made, just 9 led to the killing of an unarmed black suspect, vs. the 19 unarmed white men that were killed. Rarely, as in, white men are 25 percent MORE likely to be killed by police officers in violent acts than black people.

I could no longer stay silent. I decided to release a video discussing these truths on my Facebook page. I made it clear that despite being in the midst of committing a crime, George Floyd should not have died that day. That was not a matter of debate. Rather, he should have been properly arrested and charged. That said, I was having trouble stomaching the dishonest media portrayal of George Floyd as a "gentle giant." The journalists had refused to cover it, but Floyd himself had been a career criminal who terrorized the minority community with drugs and violence.

He had two convictions in the early 1990s for theft and the delivery of a controlled substance. He then served ten months in prison for theft with a firearm in 1998. In 2002, he was arrested for criminal trespassing and served another ten months in county jail. Later in 2002, he received an eight-month sentence for a cocaine offense, and another ten-month sentence in 2004 for a different cocaine offense. In 2005, he was charged with possession for intent to deliver a controlled substance for having more than 4 grams of cocaine, for which he served another ten months in state jail. Worst of all, came his sentencing in 2009, for an unspeakable crime he committed in 2007. Floyd, accompanied by five other male companions, pretended to be from the Water Department and forced their way inside a woman's home, while a toddler was present. The victim testified that George Floyd pressed the barrel of a loaded gun to her abdomen, while another one of his friends whipped her in the side of the head with a pistol. The men proceeded to search and rob her house of jewelry and a cell phone, although they were apparently looking for drugs. George pled guilty to the charges and was released five years later in 2012.

The mainstream media story after his death mentioned none of this. The repeated narrative was that Floyd had moved to Minneapolis for a fresh start and had been living his life as an upstanding citizen and community leader since his release. That narrative fell apart, however, when his toxicology reports returned from the medical examiner's officer. It turns out that the 911 caller was correct. Floyd was under the influence—of Fentanyl, an especially deadly, high-risk opioid that is 50 to 100 times more potent than morphine. The report determined that he also had methamphetamine in his system at the time of his death. This could perhaps explain why George Floyd uttered "I can't breathe" long before the officer placed him on the ground and placed a knee to his neck. It is alleged that video shows that George Floyd first claimed he was claustrophobic and couldn't breathe, while he was standing upright.

Nonetheless, Floyd was elevated as a hero in black America, while David Dorn, an elderly man who had lived his live admirably, was being cast aside. I was disgusted, because I knew at the root of this injustice was politics and watering that root, was a toxic culture.

My video rebuttal shocked the world. It garnered more than 100 million views in a matter of four days, and people all around the world reached out to me—thousands condemning me for speaking ill of their hero, but many more thanking me for having the courage to simply tell the whole truth. They thanked me for giving them the real statistics— for telling them that police officers are 18½ times more likely to be killed by black men than the other way around. For informing them that we do not have a "police brutality" problem in America, but we do have a black-on-black brutality problem in America, and when individuals like George Floyd are uplifted and hailed as honorable men, that problem becomes an impossible one to defeat.

Currently, the Democrat leaders in inner cities are calling for police forces to be defunded. Celebrities are backing this call. Hollywood idols and wealthy politicians can of course afford to have the police defunded because they live in gated communities and pay for private security. But can inner cities afford it? Can impoverished people afford it? Can a black woman who has her home raided by five armed men who press a gun to her belly, truly afford a world with less policing?

Black culture was once something to be proud of, but it no longer is. It has disintegrated into a web of lies and complacency. It is a perpetual diagnosis of our illnesses, running parallel to our endless denials of the antidote: the truth.

The hard truth is that the problems that exist in black America today are completely optional. We can unmarry ourselves from the toxic politicians and celebrities who further nothing but our own destruction. We can unmarry ourselves from a culture that celebrates brokenness.

Confucius also once said, "Real knowledge is knowing the extent of one's ignorance."

Take from that quotation what you will.

# 11

# ON SLAVERY

A never-ending source of political debate today surrounds the injustices of slavery and its (highly implausible) lingering effects some four hundred years later. Quite surprisingly, this topic gets the most airtime and discussion from white liberals seeking positions of power. When Elizabeth Warren, the white millionaire senator of Massachusetts, declared her candidacy for the 2020 presidential election, she also immediately declared her support for slavery reparations in a statement to Reuters: "We must confront the dark history of slavery and government-sanctioned discrimination in this country that has had many consequences including undermining the ability of black families to build wealth in America for generations."

Similarly, when Francis "Beto" O'Rourke, another white millionaire congressman from Texas, spoke before the National Action Network (a civil rights organization founded by Reverend Al Sharpton), he too declared un-equivocally his support for a House bill that would create a commission for reparations.

Presidential hopeful Bernie Sanders, also by chance a white millionaire senator from the state of Vermont, was careful not to use the word "reparations" but declared during a CNN town hall that, if elected, "we're going to do everything we can to put resources into distressed commu-nities and improve lives for those people who have been hurt by the legacy of slavery."

The presentations here are obvious: wealthy white lib-eral Democrats feel guilty about the past transgressions of white people and are looking to take corrective measures to make amends—if elected as president of the United States.

Of every position the Left takes, this one is especially irksome because it relies upon an intellectually bankrupt analysis of human history and an anachronistic view of morality.

I believe that virtually any person today who would use the argument of American slavery as a demonstration of present injustice is either sorely uneducated or manipulative. In some cases, both.

## NASTY, BRUTISH, AND SHORT

In my many speaking tours across college campuses, I began observing an odd trend among liberal students. When given an opportunity to ask me questions at the conclusion of my presentation, the students were fixated on the topic of American slavery.

I determined this to be odd, not because I was in any disagreement regarding their assessments that it was an immoral institution, but rather, because they were assigning the past transgression to white men exclusively. I began to suspect that their worldview was limited to the United States (a relatively young country with far less historical sin than many others), and with time, I found it entirely plausible that many leftists today are unaware that the world did not begin in 1619.

I do not present this theory in jest. In consideration of today's education curriculum, which has grown increasingly more focused on social issues rather than hard academics, many young students are starved of more sensible studies. As their world becomes increasingly more technological, centered on social media clicks and trending hashtags, they are becoming more literate in celebrity culture than in the much more imperative world events.

A recent example of this growing deficiency played out in early 2020, when the American government sanctioned a military operation against Iranian general Qasem Soleimani. In the immediate aftermath of his death, social media platforms began buzzing with commentary that his assassination might provoke World War III. The response from the Left, in particular, was extraordinary. After years of their radicalized feminism and claims of systemic oppression against women in America, they suddenly launched a passionate defense of the Iranian regime. In peak hysteria, actress Rose McGowan, one of the first and loudest promoters of #MeToo, tweeted, "Dear #Iran, The USA has disrespected your country, your flag, your people. 52% of us humbly apologize. We want peace with your nation. We are being held hostage by a terrorist regime. We do not know how to escape. Please do not kill us."

Those who possess even a basic understanding of the Middle Eastern region know that Iran is a country that, after the Islamic revolution of 1979, adopted a constitution which states that a woman's life is worth half that of a man. Under present Iranian law, women can be punished up to ten years in prison if they are caught in public not wearing a hijab, a headscarf that must cover all of their hair and most of their skin. Among many other restrictions, women are not allowed to watch male sports in stadiums and are routinely imprisoned for speaking out in protest of discriminations.

But before there was time to wrap our heads around the Left's dizzying about-face on women's issues, another tweet went out from Colin Kaepernick, the former American football quarterback turned leader of the national anthem protests against the already-debunked myth of police brutality. His tweet read: "There is nothing new about American attacks against Black and Brown people for the expansion of American imperialism. America has always sanctioned and besieged Black and Brown bodies both at home and abroad. America militarism is the weapon wielded by American imperialism, to enforce its policing and plundering of the nonwhite world."

This arrived as definitive proof that Kaepernick either does not know the definition of imperialism or is utterly ignorant regarding the history of Iran. Because Iran, of course, has been around since long before the United States, and up until 1935 it used to be known as Persia. And while Persia was known for many things, it was certainly never considered within the context of American imperialism. In fact, and rather unfortunately for Colin's narrative, Persia is perhaps most notorious for its empire—a literal imperial dynasty—that lasted for two hundred years (almost as long as America has been a country!). The Persians imperialized regions from Egypt to India. They were once the most powerful state in the world.

The history of the Persians is not limited to textbooks either. Their brutal period of invasions is so well known it was even brought to the big screen in the 2006 blockbuster film *300*, a fictionalized retelling of the ruthless Persian "God-King" Xerxes and his armies' attempt to conquer the Greeks. Is it possible that Kaepernick was truly ignorant, or were his motives more sinister? A deeper look into his history of racialized tweets suggests the latter.

On Thanksgiving Day of 2019 Kaepernick signified that he had spent the morning at a Native American "Un-Thanksgiving" ceremony. He tweeted, "the U.S. Government has stolen over 1.5 billion acres of land from Indigenous people. Thank you to my indigenous family. I am with you today and always," along with footage of him celebrating with a tribe. In the same vein, earlier that same year on the Fourth of July he tweeted, "what to the American slave, is your fourth of July?"—co-opting a Frederick Douglass speech that was given *before* the Civil War formally ended slavery. It should be noted that Frederick Douglass, a former slave who went on to become one of the most prolific abolitionist writers of his day, also wrote in that same speech about the "genius of American institutions." His speech was an effort to encourage America to rid itself of the horrible practice of slavery so that it could move forward to become the glorious country that he believed in. Despite Kaepernick's portrayal, Frederick Douglass was very much an American patriot. Stripping the quote of its context and repurposing it long after slavery's abolition was an act of pure deceit. It is exactly the sort of anachronistic behavior that the Left routinely engages in, in their efforts to portray false equivalencies.

Kaepernick's tweets eternally convict America. He portrays the United States as a fundamentally immoral country, which will never be absolved of its early sins. This is the very sentiment perpetuated by many leftists and liberals who deem it mission-critical to right those wrongs.

But their sentiments are entirely rubbish, because slavery did not begin with colonial white European men in America. Rather, it existed everywhere in the world since the dawn of humanity. Therefore, and as a point of ideological consistency regarding the purportedly immortal shame of the practice, Kaepernick should not have been celebrating with Native Americans. Because they too once practiced slavery. Yes, it's an inconvenient truth, but indigenous tribes were not sitting around kumbaya-ing over a fireplace, as leftists would have us believe. Rather, they were attempting to imperialize one another. They would enslave their war captives into labor and in many instances would utilize torture as a part of their religious rites. And it gets worse.

Before Europeans ever landed in the Americas, Native Americans routinely cannibalized one another. Most notorious among them, perhaps, were the Aztecs. When the Spanish colonists arrived in Mexico City, they were greeted by arranged piles of more than 100,000 skulls belonging to human beings who had been sacrificed to the gods.

In one archaeological expedition, they discovered the remains of forty-two children, all around the age of five, who were sacrificed to the rain god. Special ceremonies required more sacrifice. On the inauguration of the Aztec's Templo Mayor, they sacrificed between 20,000 and 60,000 human beings.

Relying upon the research of Mexican-American Harvard historian David Carrasco, author Rodney Stark recounted the Aztec ceremonial practices in his book *How the West Won*:

> *The ceremonies . . . were performed in front of large crowds. An adult male victim usually was held down on a sacrificial stone atop a pyramid, his chest was slashed open, and the priest snatched his still beating heart and held it aloft to the sun. The head of the victim was usually severed and placed on a rack—soon to be a skull added to the ceremonial collection. Then [the remaining body] was rolled, flailing down the temple steps to the bottom where it was skinned and dismembered. The choice cuts were distributed to onlookers, who took them home and ate them.*

Despite the fact that early colonialists wrote extensively about the savage culture of Native Americans, their writings were eventually dismissed in the name of political correctness. The preferred narrative was that white European men needed to savagely portray the indigenous people to justify their own genocidal pursuits. It was even assumed that the Native Americans themselves had lied, or rather, had been *misunderstood* in their own recorded sacred texts regarding their practices.

That is, until science. Eventual anthropological studies determined conclusively that Native Americans, just as Christopher Columbus and so many early colonists had first reported, routinely engaged in cannibalism. Today, this truth is no longer a matter of dispute. However reluctantly, even the left-wing *New York Times* published an article citing scientific evidence of indigenous cannibalism in Colorado, and the Smithsonian now formally acknowledges that northwest Native Americans practiced slavery. According to the Standard Cross-Cultural Files, at least thirty-nine indigenous societies practiced slavery, just as brutally and immorally as everywhere else. Yet for whatever reason, the sum of their slavery and cannibalism is not problematic for the Left, or at least, not *as problematic* as the white man's slavery. So just why is it that the Left wants us to look the other way? Why is it that in their view, imperialism, cannibalism, murder, slavery, and every other undeniably sinful act become forgivable, so long as it was not executed by white men?

By no means do I intend to offer some sweeping condemnation of Native American tribes, nor do I intend to vindicate the actions of early colonialists. My purpose here is to simply tell the truth, and the truth is that human history is complicated and no men, regardless of skin complexion, stand guiltless.

Yet today black Americans are never told to consider the murderous Persian Empire or the cannibalism of indigenous tribes, or the heinous actions under the imperialistic Egyptian Empire, the Turkish Empire, the Muslim Abbasid and Rashidun Caliphate Empires, the Chinese Yuan or Ming Empires, the Mongol Empire, the Ottoman Empire, or the Japanese Empire, to name just a few. Black Americans are taught to believe that historical sin is almost synonymous with white men; the white man's history and the white man's history only is to be loathed.

Yet another inconvenient truth for leftists is the fact that the much-despised white men were, in fact, the first to formally abolish slavery. In 1833, Britain was the first country in the history of the world to pass a Slavery Abolition Act. They were quickly followed by France, who in 1848 re-abolished slavery to include her many colonies. Then of course came the Thirteenth Amendment to the United States Constitution. After centuries of human slavery, white men led the world in putting an end to the abhorrent practice.

But there is hardly an honest discussion about the conclusion of slavery. Similarly, there is hardly a fruitful dialogue regarding the seventeenth-century world—a far departure from the modernized society that we enjoy today. It was a place perhaps best captured by the words of Thomas Hobbes in a 1651 treatise. Hobbes describes a world of "no arts, no letters, no society; and which is worst of all, continual fear, and danger of violent death. And the life of a man, solitary, poor, nasty, brutish and short."

## BACK TO AFRICA

I have encountered many young black students who lament to me about all that was taken from us when the evil white men took us from our original lands. I have yet to find a single one of these students who can name for me which African country they wish to live in today. Although they'd never admit to it, there is tacit awareness that however ugly our method of ancestral transportation, we are blessed beyond reason to have inherited the freedom to live in America today.

Stranger still, there is a smaller faction of black youth who are under the impression that we descended from kings and queens. Often, I come across extraordinary depictions on social media, that Africans were all enjoying the status of pharaohs before Europeans came and laid waste to their paradise.

Oh, how I wish this were true. It's just that it isn't.

The truth is that Africans were sold into slavery by other Africans. And the more horrifying particulars are that in many cases, we were sold for items as basic as gin and mirrors. Our lives had very little value to our ancestors then and upon the continent of Africa today; they hold very little value there.

Despite being a half-white man who was adopted and raised by two white parents, Colin Kaepernick never misses an opportunity to exploit African victimhood. This is perhaps why on the Fourth of July 2019, he tweeted, "How can we truly celebrate independence on a day that intentionally robbed our ancestors of theirs? To find my independence I went home." He was referring, of course, to Africa. Kaepernick made the decision to travel to Ghana because, by his own account, "he wanted to see what his people saw" before they were forcefully taken away.

I really want to drive this point home, so allow me to restate the parameters: In lieu of celebrating his independence in America, Colin Kaepernick went to Africa, a continent upon which he found better grounds for celebration. And what an interesting venue for celebration it was, because when it comes to the topic of independence, there are currently close to 700,000 slaves in Africa today and, remarkably, they are being enslaved by other Africans. Child soldiers, human trafficking, forced labor—these are the current conditions that exist within the same sub-Saharan region where the transatlantic slave trade originated. Africans bodies are being sold today like they were sold then—and no, they are not being purchased by any country of white men. In fact, slavery today is *exclusively* practiced within nonwhite countries. In other words, there is not a single majority-white country that has institutionalized slavery today. There is a lot that can be said about the verifiable benefits of European colonialism all over the world, but we will leave that thesis for another day.

Ghana is an especially ironic country to plan an emotional reprieve from American celebrations because there are currently twenty thousand children enslaved to support the fishing industry along Lake Volta. Left-wing news network CNN covered the tragedy in 2019. They interviewed a young boy who was rescued from enslavement about what he had been made to endure. He explained to them that while in captivity, "we worked tirelessly. And if you'd go for a small fish to satisfy your hunger, they'd beat you so badly, you'd regret ever coming into the world."

So why was Ghana such a comforting country for Colin Kaepernick? And why haven't any of the alleged "courageous leaders" on black issues of oppression mentioned any of the horrific present-day circumstances in Africa? Surely the mere knowledge of the dire economic and physical conditions forced upon Africans today might lead many of the black youth to feel grateful for the many freedoms afforded to them in America, so why don't black "leaders" like Al Sharpton or Jesse Jackson wish to inspire such patriotism?

The answer is simple. Because they wouldn't profit from patriotism. Black victimhood is profitable. It elects politicians to their seats and funds organizations, like the NAACP, that are committed to "exposing" (read: exploiting) racism, for a nominal fee. In essence, black Americans are now being extorted by various individuals and groups who rake in millions by pretending to be allies to a fleeting cause. Should black Americans no longer view themselves as separate from the American dream and should black Americans embody the patriotic spirit, many race hustlers would be put out of business.

## DEMOCRAT PLANTATIONS

There is another biblical quote that I am quite fond of because its wisdom cannot be overstated. "What has been will be again. What has been done will be done again. There is nothing new beneath the sun" (Ecclesiastes 1:9).

In January 2018, the *Washington Post* published a hit piece about me titled "How the 'Democratic Plantation' became one of conservatives' favorite slurs." In it, the author asserts that "comparisons between chattel slavery and contemporary black politics are deeply flawed, and add little to contemporary understanding . . . like slaves before them, black voters have agency and are not mindless cogs in the Democratic machine."

The purpose of the article was to insinuate that the phrase "Democrat Plantation," as popularized by me, is an insulting and baseless comparison that ought to be rejected. What the author fails to note, however, is that in no way had I intended for "Democrat Plantation" to be used as a mere catchphrase. Each time I utter it, I mean it in its literal interpretation.

Let's consider, in layman's terms, what exactly the institution of American slavery brought upon the Africans who were sold into it.

✦ In 1860, just before the start of the American Civil War, 4 million black Americans were enslaved by white Democrats. As a matter of housekeeping—almost no Republicans ever owned a slave. The barbaric practice was put into effect to benefit white Democrats economically; blacks were made to work like animals on southern plantations. They labored from sunrise to sunset at *absolutely no benefit to themselves.*

+ As previously discussed, slavery also carried with it the systemic breakdown of family, as slaves were continually separated and auctioned away from their loved ones.

+ Slave work was done under threat of physical abuse. Any slave who made an attempt to escape the plantation was met with the worst forms of punishment: sometimes they were whipped within an inch of their lives, other times their limbs were severed to discourage repeat behavior, and in the worst of circumstances, recaptured slaves were murdered as a severe warning to other slaves not to disobey.

+ State laws stipulated that it was illegal for slaves to learn to read and write. Illiteracy was so crucial to the institution of slavery that even white men faced fines and imprisonment if they were discovered teaching blacks to read. The purpose of such laws was obvious: it is difficult to control an educated mind. Slave owners rightfully feared that slaves who could read might come across the abolitionist writings that were in circulation from the North. Awareness of the nation's growing sympathy to their freedom surely might have inspired slaves to rebel against their owners.

American slavery, then, was an institution that was run by white Democrats, relied upon black work, and demanded family breakdown, threats of abuse, and illiteracy.

So what exactly has changed? Certainly not the results. Perhaps all that has been amended are the means by which today's Democrats achieve those results.

Today, black voters are considered the backbone of the Democrat Party, and for good reason. In 2012, Barack Obama received 93 percent of the black vote. Exit polls from the 2016 presidential election revealed that 88 percent of black voters supported Hillary Clinton. This 5 percent dip was a critical factor in Clinton's loss to Donald Trump and represents a dangerous trend for Democrats, who would face an existential crisis if they lost another 5 percent in

2020. Not a single expert denies that there is absolutely no path to victory for Democrats if Republicans are able to peel off 20 percent of the black vote. It is therefore true to state that Democrats rely upon the black vote for success. It is also true that, just as in the time of slavery, the work we do for them is done at absolutely no benefit to us, as our communities continue to face criminal, economic, and moral decline.

On the topic of family breakdown, we have covered extensively the impact of the 1960s Great Society upon the black family. Not yet discussed is the manner in which this epidemic extraordinarily impacts the psyche of our youth. For the plantation owners of days past, breaking down the family carried more than just a financial incentive of buying the stronger slaves and auctioning off the weakest ones. The psychological effects upon the slave were also beneficial, and is perhaps best detailed by Frederick Douglass in his autobiography, *Narrative of the Life of Frederick Douglass*:

> *Never having enjoyed, to any considerable extent, her soothing presence, her tender and watchful care, I received the tidings of her death with much the same emotions I should have probably felt at the death of a stranger . . . the ties that ordinarily bind children to their homes were*

*all suspended in my case. I found no severe trial in my departure. My home was charmless; it was not home to me; on parting from it, I could not feel that I was leaving anything which I could have enjoyed by staying.*

Douglass's lack of emotion when he learned of his mother's death and lack of emotion in leaving the only home he ever knew are fascinating to consider. The eventual result of his family's breakdown is a dehumanized response to what most would consider a life-altering trauma. It becomes apparent that if slaveholders wanted their captives to remain emotionless in the face of their ever-changing circumstances, denying them early love and affection was crucial. It becomes even clearer how the same strategy of early dehumanization via systemic breakdown is leading to a culture of crime and immorality.

## ALLEGORY OF THE DEMOCRAT CAVE

On the point of illiteracy, we covered in chapter 6 the many ways in which the public education system is failing black students and how a lack of education can create cultural sheep: individuals who vote and think according to how their favorite rappers and singers tell them they ought to.

In considering the necessity of illiteracy to maintain slavery, I am reminded of the Greek philosopher Plato's famed "Allegory of the Cave," as presented in his most famous work, *The Republic*. The parable forces us to imagine a group of prisoners who have been imprisoned since childhood in a cave. They are chained in such a way that they cannot see one another, themselves, or anything beyond the wall in front of them. There is a fire that blazes behind the prisoners, and therefore, casts shadows onto the wall in front of them. Various different objects that are held by people who walk behind the prisoners cast different shadows. Plato suggests that with time, the shadows become the prisoners' reality, for they know no other existence beyond what is put in front of them in the cave. Simply put, reality is determined by knowledge, or lack thereof.

But Plato then imagines what might happen if one of those prisoners was freed. What would happen if after years of processing reality, as it were, a prisoner escaped toward the light outside the cave? Plato supposes that the prisoner would naturally reject the light. The sunlight would bring pain to the prisoner's eyes, angering and blinding him in such a dramatic way that he would naturally retreat back into the dark comfort of the cave.

The anger, the blindness—this so perfectly encapsulates

the state of so many black Americans who remain committed to the cave of the Democrat Party, seemingly beyond reason. It has more to do with comfort and familiarity. The great big world outside the cave can seem initially daunting. It is easier to retreat back into the reality that has been so carefully constructed for us.

But then Plato supposes another scenario. What if the prisoner is dragged out, against his will, unable to retreat for comfort? Plato reckons that the sun would overwhelm and blind the prisoner at first, but then, "slowly, his eyes adjust to the light of the sun. First, he can only see shadows. Gradually he can see the reflections of people and things in water and then later see the people and things themselves. Eventually, he is able to look at the stars and moon at night until finally he can look upon the sun itself," and only then is he "able to reason about [the sun]" and what it is.

Now armed with a more complete education of the world outside the cave, Plato surmises the prisoner would become overwhelmed with the blessing of his freedom and naturally want to bring the remaining prisoners into the light.

Easier said than done.

Because the remaining prisoners, when confronted with

the truth, would ridicule the truth-teller. Plato suggests that the free prisoner, now having been exposed to the light for a long period, would have difficulty readjusting his eyes instantly back to the cave's darkness. The remaining prisoners would conclude "that [the prisoner] had gone up but only in order to come back down to the cave with his eyes ruined—and thus it certainly does not pay to go up." Plato concludes that the remaining prisoners would rather kill a person who attempted to force them from their chains than find themselves subjected to the same blinding sun.

It is a remarkable story with a timeless truth. Though written in 514 B.C., it is a demonstration of why slave owners more than one thousand years later sought to limit education: because education is sunlight. Today in California, arguably the most liberal state in the United States, 75 percent of black boys cannot pass the state literacy exam. With literacy being used once again as a means of social control and oppression, it is an additional hurdle for black conservatives—those of us who have seen the light—to invite our brothers and sisters into reality. If one seeks to control a group of people, all aspects of any narrative they come across must be dominated. Under dominant Democrat leadership, blacks are not meant to even consider another way of existing in this world. Many would figuratively kill rather than see themselves dragged into a different state of being.

## MODERN LYNCHING

While it is obvious to many that the broken institutions of family and education can fertilize consequences reminiscent of the time of slavery, the topic of punishment is not as conspicuous.

With the abolishment of slavery, so too went the legal right to punish blacks physically, but for Democrats, that simply indicated that they needed to get more creative. Draped in long white robes and hoods, Klansmen aimed to resist the Republican Party's Reconstruction-era policies, which sought to establish political and economic equality for blacks. Klan members used a variety of intimidation tactics against black and white Republican activists and, eventually, against immigrants, Catholics, and Jewish people as well. The Democrat terrorist group would go on to lynch 3,446 black Republicans, and 1,297 white Republicans, all in the name of preserving the "moral good" of white supremacy. Presumably, all of this came to a screeching halt with the passing of the Civil Rights Act.

*But there is nothing new beneath the sun.*

Modernized, updated, more developed, perhaps, but nothing new. Indeed, once again, the Democrats have simply become more creative.

Freedom can exist only in the absence of punishment for our choices. If blacks voting for Democrats today is simply an act of freedom (as the aforementioned *Washington Post* article suggested), then there should be no evidence of punishment for blacks who choose to vote otherwise.

Unfortunately, that is not the case. Instead, when a black American gathers the agency to walk away from the Democrats and publicly announces the reasons as to why, the punishment that awaits is severe and is inflicted by the hands of our mainstream media. Of course, it would be unconscionable for the Democrats to chain and whip their runaways publicly. Today they use the less detectable tools of slander and libel, in an effort to leave black conservatives within an inch of their professional (and sometimes personal) lives.

Few people know this as well as I do.

If you feed it my name, Google's search engine will return over 10 million hits. I have been made to undergo an increasingly bizarre and excruciatingly public autopsy, ever since I outed myself as a black conservative. Journalists spent time detailing how much I was paid at every single event I was invited to speak at in 2017. There are articles posing inquiry into whether I have ever dated black men, plus articles about my husband, my net worth, and what my eighty-year-old grandfather likely thinks about me.

If you averaged the sum of all of the links that returned after searching my name, you would be operating under the assumption that Candace Owens is at best an out-of-touch conservative afforded too much privilege in life to understand the struggles of her own community, or at worst—and despite what extraordinary ideological leaps you'd have to make to arrive at such a point with conviction—you would have me pegged as another white supremacist who, rather inconveniently, happens to be black.

There is seemingly no stone leftist journalists are willing to leave unturned in their wild pursuit to portray me as someone that I simply am not. I have since learned that the Left would much sooner believe in the paranormal, like the existence of black people who are supporters of white supremacy, than in the much more logical existence of black conservatism. In this same vein, the accusation that Dr. Ben Carson (a *literal* brain surgeon) is somehow "stupid" has become the dominating theory among left-wing critics who prefer not to process the rather uncomplicated fact that he is simply both black *and* Republican.

Indeed, via false media narratives, some of the most accomplished black men and women of our time—Dr. Condoleezza Rice, Dr. Thomas Sowell, Supreme Court justice Clarence Thomas, Larry Elder—are routinely attacked as blacks who simply hate their own skin. This is the morally preferred strategy that society has landed upon today; black Republicans are still to be terrorized, but not in the same conspicuous manner of the past.

The role of left-wing journalism is to sanction, through its routine attacks and dehumanizing coverage of black conservatives, the public shaming, ostracism, and sometimes violence that we are made to endure. Journalists grant social clemency. It becomes acceptable to viciously pursue blacks who refuse to bend to the will of Democrats.

As for severing the limbs of runaway slaves, the purpose of such smearing is a figurative dismembering. The Left's intention is to make it impossible for outspoken black conservatives to move forward in their careers. Where will we work? Who will give us a platform? Who in the world would welcome an individual accused of something as heinous as white supremacy?

Fortunately, like many others who have come before me, I have survived every media assassination attempt, but not without, as was intended, an increase in threats being made against me by the Left's domestic terrorist group— Antifa. Clad in all-black clothing and black masks (a more modern take on the fashion of their spiritual predecessors, the Ku Klux Klansmen), their members arrive in swarms to bully, harass, intimidate, and beat conservatives in public places.

In August 2018, I was eating breakfast at a café in Philadelphia with my colleague Charlie Kirk. Having recognized us in the restaurant, about forty Antifa members assembled outside. A few of them came into the restaurant and began shouting at us to leave. Police officers were called to the scene to safely deliver us from the restaurant. When we got outside, the gang members began screaming obscenities, throwing eggs and water at us. We were fortunate to capture the entire incident on camera. For many liberals, it became a wake-up call to what their party had become: white gangs chasing black Republicans out of restaurants in the name of protecting the values of Democrats. *What has been will be again.*

One would think that such routine displays of blatant bigotry and violence would be roundly condemned by all media members, but that is not the case. Instead, Antifa is hailed as a heroic force by leftist media figures. In fact, the prevailing mainstream narrative of the day, just as it was when the Klansmen brutalized blacks, is that certain forms of violence ought to be sanctioned for the greater moral good of society."

It was CNN anchor Chris Cuomo who during a live broadcast offered a defense of Antifa's lawlessness when he declared, "It's not about being right in the eyes of the law, but you also have to know what's right and wrong in a moral—in a good and evil sense . . . that's why people who show up to fight against bigots are not to be judged the same as the bigots, even if they do resort to the same kinds of petty violence."

Cuomo is offering that violence against people who, according to his own moral view, are the *real* problem is justifiable. Antifa then is acting just as the Klan were in their day: as humble guardians of a more righteous narrative.

It becomes clear then how through slander, libel, and media-sanctioned violence, the Democrats have not halted but merely updated their methods of abuse against black Americans who wander off their plantation of thought. Clarence Thomas may have described this reality best in his 1991 Senate confirmation hearing. Facing mounting pressure to withdraw his Supreme Court nomination due to unsubstantiated sexual harassment allegations that, rather conveniently, arose against him, Thomas testified: "From my standpoint as a black American, as far as I'm concerned, it is a high-tech lynching for uppity blacks who in any way deign to think for themselves, to do for themselves, to have different ideas, and it is a message that unless you kowtow to an old order, this is what will happen to you. You will be lynched, destroyed, caricatured . . . rather than hung from a tree."

Despite the illusion of freedom, black Americans are just as I said—still on a plantation. And the more popular that black conservatives bringing news of the abolitionist movement up north become, the more feverishly our media establishment attempts to whip us out of existence.

The dark intentions of the Democrat Party have simply metamorphosed.

## FREEDOM

It was Thomas Paine's pamphlet *Common Sense* that laid the groundwork and emboldened the colonists to take up arms and fight for independence from the British monarchy. It is my hope that this book, in the hands of every black American, might lay down a similar path for revolution.

True freedom and real change are always possible. I awake every morning with a renewed sense of hope that we are moving closer and closer to dragging Plato's prisoners into the light. I have learned to practice patience, persistence, and optimism through my admiration of Frederick Douglass, who once wrote, "I have seen how a man was made a slave." His words ring like a timeless bell because I believe that I too have seen how men are made slaves. I have seen how black Americans have been enslaved by the debate of race. I have seen how liberals and leftists, under guidance from the Democrat establishment, have stripped us of our families, our faith, and our futures. But Douglass's quotation continues, with a promising forewarning:

"And now you shall see how a slave was made a man."

And so we shall.

# CONCLUSION

After the 2016 election, liberal America collectively mourned Hilary Clinton's loss. In an interesting post-analysis, many prominent leaders issued condemnations to black Americans who declined to vote, thereby depriving Hillary of her much-assumed win. The accusation was that those who had not voted took for granted the privileges afforded to them by their ancestors' pain and suffering.

The insinuation was appalling: that when wealthy elitist career politicians do not get what they want, it is because black people failed them.

Far from a call for black Americans to exercise their

rights, this admonishment represented a reminder that our votes are seen as little more than our duty—not to ourselves, but to the almighty liberal establishment. The implication was clear: black Americans at polling stations are not assumed to be making a choice but rather delivering a guarantee: a guarantee to the Democrat Party that we will unquestionably commit ourselves to their continued empowerment.

The current state of affairs gives the impression that black men, women, and children sacrificed their lives to give modern blacks the opportunity to support Democrats in perpetuity. But the truth is that blood spilled by our ancestors was spilled for our freedom. Our complete freedom: the freedom to vote for and support *any* candidate of our choosing.

We have the right—no, the *obligation*—to think for ourselves, untethered by the assumptions that the liberal establishment places upon us.

I fight for black America to wake up to this freedom. To have the courage to walk away when any one person or political party no longer serves us.

In late 2018, I launched BLEXIT (Black + Exit), a movement dedicated to driving conservative principles into minority communities. My mission is simple: to challenge black America to rise to our potential. It's not always easy to swim against the current. I am a walking testament to what happens if you dare to make an escape, once again, from the Democrat plantations.

It can be difficult to stand by the faith of your personal convictions, especially when most of the world seems to be raised against you.

The criticism I receive comes from every angle. When I speak to minority audiences, many will say to me, "Candace, I can get with you on all of the conservative stuff, but Trump? REALLY?!"

Really. Because it could have been no one else.

Who else but a boisterous New Yorker would have the courage to stand up to the entire liberal establishment? Who else but Donald J. Trump would have the courage to look black America in the face and ask us what we had to lose?

"No group in America has been more harmed by Hillary Clinton's policies than African Americans; no group," he said. "If Hillary Clinton's goal was to inflict pain on the African American community, she could not have done a better job. It's a disgrace. Tonight, I'm asking for the vote of every single African American in this country who wants to see a better future. . . . Look how much African American communities have suffered under Democrat control. To

those I say the following: What do you have to lose by trying something new like Trump? . . . America must reject the
bigotry of Hillary Clinton, who sees communities of color
only as votes, not as human beings worthy of a better future."

Trump's words forced an immediate awakening upon
me. I was stunned by the lack of etiquette—by his unapologetic nerve to tell the truth. In that exact moment, I realized
something: if black America was going to turn the corner
on the poverty, miseducation, and broken families that have
loomed large for the last sixty years, it had to be him.

It had to be somebody with no political experience. It
had to be someone from the outside, who came into our
political china shop like a raging bull. It was never going to
work any other way for black America, because when you
systematically remove authority and structure from the
homes, you create a group of individuals who do not respond well to traditional authority. If we are being honest,
black America was never going to respond to etiquette. We
are the most politically incorrect group in America: the
group who birthed hip-hop and pushed American culture
away from its more buttoned-up inclinations.

As a result, we needed someone equally as disruptive
and against the status quo. We needed to get what we had
been giving: someone who goes against the grain and will

not allow faux outrage to shrink his ambitions. The black community had been dying a slow death aided by political correctness. We had accepted poise and politeness over honest dialogue. We had learned to accept lies and victimhood over truth and victorhood. And so we needed someone who could figuratively shake us back to reality.

What I love about Donald Trump is his audacity—the sheer audacity he has to tell people the truth even when he is being smeared, libeled, threatened, and told to reverse his statements. It is the same audacity that he displayed when standing on a stage in the upper Midwest and challenging all black Americans to stop pretending that we were okay when we were not. We were not winning because Obama was in the White House. In fact, by nearly every metric, we were losing. In addition to Trump's reference to dismal inner-city schools and high unemployment among blacks, there is the fact that, during Obama's presidency, black wealth took a stunning downturn. Matt Bruenig, founder of the People's Policy Project, and journalist Ryan Cooper discussed this issue in a 2017 essay written for *Jacobin* magazine titled "How Obama Destroyed Black Wealth":

*The Obama presidency was a disaster for middle-class wealth in the United States. Between 2007 and 2016,* *the average wealth of the bottom 99 percent dropped by $4,500. Over the same period, the average wealth of the top 1 percent rose by $4.9 million.*

*This drop hit the housing wealth of African Americans particularly hard. Outside of home equity, black wealth recovered its 2007 level by 2016. But average black home equity was still $16,700 lower.*

*Much of this decline, we will argue, can be laid at the feet of President Obama. His housing policies led directly to millions of families losing their homes. What's more, Obama had the power—money, legislative tools, and legal leverage—to sharply ameliorate the foreclosure crisis.*

*He chose not to use it.*

To many, Hillary should have won the 2016 presidential election because of goodness. It would have been *good* to say that we elected of our first female president, and that goodness would have certainly reverberated throughout the world as a symbol of progressive glory. Similarly, it was *good* when we elected President Barack Obama, the first black man to serve as the leader of the free world. Likewise, because truth serves as a secondary aspiration to goodness, it is not acceptable to discuss that, despite his blackness, President Barack Obama failed black America. But in the end, truth always catches up to goodness.

This explains why, despite the *good* promise of socialism, Venezuela has erupted into chaos. It also explains why, despite sixty years of *good* government policies and *good* promises made by leftist politicians, black America has not seen much improvement. The goodness of welfare and affirmative action has been met with the reality that there is no substitute for hard work. And this is why Donald Trump, despite being subjected to despicable treatment from the mainstream media, who claim to uphold all that is *good*, has done more for black America than any politician in recent memory.

## THE TRUTH ABOUT TRUMP

I am convinced that many black Americans are opposed to Trump because they simply do not understand who he is. The mainstream media has bombarded us with messaging about his flaws and indiscretions—as if leftists are somehow inherently holy—yet they fail to shed light on the true value that he brings to the presidency. And while I believe that Trump's aggressive persona is necessary if we are going to see true progress in the black community and America as a whole, I understand that it can rub some people the wrong way. As a result, many people are blinded by their ignorance.

So let us discuss who President Trump actually is. We all know that he is a real estate mogul, turned TV star, turned president of the United States. But beyond that, I believe that Trump represents the best kind of civil upheaval, a shattering of the status quo not unlike the Hebrew slaves' ancient Exodus from Egypt, America's birth via the Revolutionary War, or the Allies' defeat of Nazism and then the Soviet Union. Since the end of the Cold War, globalist, neoliberal policies have crystallized a system that served only politicians, because it was built *by* politicians. And since he made his dramatic entry onto the political stage, Trump has worked valiantly to upend this deeply entrenched, self-obsessed, elite globalist order.

This shift has not come without consequence, of course. As with any chemical reaction, even if you achieve the desired results, you are often left with an undesirable by-product. In Trump's case, the first by-product was the clear crystallization of the leftist agenda: the false pretense that racism, xenophobia, misogyny, or homophobia were anything more than catchphrases used to insult and denigrate conservatives, while holding hostage black Americans and other minority groups. The second by-product was the total transformation of the mainstream media into leftist puppets and masters of psychological and emotional manipulation. And the third, thoroughly unsurprising, by-product has been the Democrat response to Trump's presidency. Like all rulers of the past whose authority was challenged, the Left has sought to delegitimize the election of the president by any means possible.

But a tiger backed into a corner always roars loudest and fights hardest. Indeed, the real #TimesUp movement has been Trump's commitment to remain on the front lines of such frivolous attacks while continuing to fight for liberty, justice, and truth and, most important, for those who have been long ignored by the liberal political machine. For a black community that has been tokenized and leveraged for the personal gain of a select few, Trump's actions are a welcome relief.

Even if they had pledged to forgo their long-standing Democrat allegiance, the black community was never going to respond to Mitt Romney, Paul Ryan, or John McCain, candidates who lacked the tenacity to upset the establishment in the name of freedom. Black America needed someone who was a cultural firebrand, someone who was unafraid to look his voters and his opposition in the eye and tell them exactly what they needed to hear: truth.

Today, the black community finally has a president who is willing to stand on the stage and say that the worst thing facing black America is not "white supremacy" but failing schools, not "police racism" but father absence, not a racist job market but a welfare system that discourages hard work and self-sufficiency. Despite the explosive reaction to his presidency, Trump has sought to expose the lies of the Left that have deceived black America for years, thereby leading to our community's great awakening.

Moreover, Trump's defense of the Constitution and upholding of the rights and liberties of the American individual is, indeed, making America great again. I said what I said. The fact that so many people, including black Americans, respond to Trump's brilliant campaign slogan by asking when America was ever great is a testament to the effectiveness of liberal propaganda. Again, I am not denying any of the atrocities that black people have faced in this country. But without the radical, freethinking innovation of the Constitution of the United States, we would likely still be enslaved. Certainly, it was the founding principles of this country—freedom and liberty for all under God—that served as a moral compass for our Founding Fathers, even when they chose not to follow it. And it is those principles that created the space for black

Americans to achieve incredible success just a few years after living in bondage.

Regarding black America specifically, the preservation of the Constitution is essential to our continued freedom, for should that document be trampled on and discarded—as are so many constitutions across the world—it is inarguable that we would bear the heaviest burden. Like black men who become the first casualties of an overzealous feminist movement and black children who suffer most at the hands of inadequate schools, black Americans can ill afford to see the rights and liberties of any Americans questioned.

In his inaugural speech, Trump spoke directly to his commitment to making America great again, not just for some people, but for *all* Americans—the forgotten ones, and the ones who have forgotten how great America is:

> *The forgotten men and women of our country will be forgotten no longer. Everyone is listening to you now. You came by the tens of millions to become part of a historic movement the likes of which the world has never seen before. At the center of this movement is a crucial conviction: that a nation exists to serve its citizens. Americans want great schools for their children, safe neighborhoods for their families, and good*

*jobs for themselves. These are the just and reasonable demands of a righteous public. But for too many of our citizens, a different reality exists: mothers and children trapped in poverty in our inner cities; rusted-out factories scattered like tombstones across the landscape of our nation; an education system, flush with cash, but which leaves our young and beautiful students deprived of knowledge; and the crime and gangs and drugs that have stolen too many lives and robbed our country of so much unrealized potential.*

What power those words have—uniting all those across this country to aim for the common goal of a restored America and tying us into a global movement of popular revolution that is sweeping away the diseased old liberal establishment.

In my opening chapter I asked what it meant to be a black *American*. The answer? Exactly the same as a white, Latino, Asian, or Jewish American. All groups have their own story to tell, and ours is one marked with suffering and tragedy, yet triumph through strength. In modern America, we are all afforded the same opportunities, the same chances to make something of ourselves, the same potential to turn our lives, no matter how humble the beginnings, into ones of significance in whatever form that may be. That is the vision of the Constitution, that was the vision of the Founding Fathers, and that must be the aspirational peak of young Americans, no matter what creed or color.

For too long we have let these dreams and hopes be dictated to us by those who seek to keep us mentally enslaved. St. Paul writes in his Letter to the Galatians, "For freedom Christ has set us free; stand firm therefore, and do not submit again to a yoke of slavery"—how potent these words still seem today, thousands of years after they were written. A people who had been set free then voluntarily chose to resubmit themselves to slavery, not in the physical sense of chains and bondage, but in the even more powerful sense of being mentally captured. This mental slavery, like some sort of twisted Stockholm syndrome, demands its addictive fix every four years, when our slave masters come rattling our cages, corralling us to pledge our permanent sacrifice: vote for us and your life will be easy; accept your victimhood.

People tell me I am a fighter, so here is my call to arms: black America, break free and do not look back. More and more are crossing into the Promised Land; join them. Once you discover the incredible power of realizing that you are answerable only to yourself and God and that no politician owns you, no politically correct agenda dictates to you, no ideology subjugates you, no history binds you, and, yes, no one political party controls your vote—then you have found freedom.

If black America finds its free voice, if there is a black-out from the liberal establishment, and if the occasional voices of those freed from the mental slavery of the Left turn, instead, into a chorus, then black America will finally find that its suffering may turn a corner. The real issues facing our community will be answered, and we will see the beauty and richness of our history as well as the promise and vision of our future. In President Trump we have the beginning. The gates of the liberal castle are under attack; we must now batter them down and storm the fortress of the liberal order.

Join the ideological battle now.

Let us turn the lights off in the liberal establishments of America as we shut the door behind us.

Let us make this blackout a reality.

# NOTES

## FOREWORD BY LARRY ELDER

xiv Walter Williams quote: "Black Families and the Welfare State," YouTube video, :50, posted by LibertyPen, November 8, 2013, https://www.youtu.be.com/YzNYCPZXvlw.

xiv Moynihan Report: Daniel Patrick Moynihan, "The Negro Family: The Case for National Action," Office of Policy Planning and Research, United States Department of Labor, March 1965, https://web.stanford.edu/~mrosenfe/Moynihan's%20The%20Negro%20Family.pdf.

xv CDC report: Centers for Disease Control and Prevention, National Center for Health Statistics, "Number and Percent of Births to Unmarried Women, by Race and Hispanic Origin: United States, 1940–2000," https://www.cdc.gov/nchs/data/statab/t001x17.pdf.

xvii *Time*/CNN poll: Associated Press, "Most black teenagers say racism has little effect on day-to-day lives," *Deseret News*, Novem-

ber 17, 1997, https://www.deseret.com/1997/11/17/19346193
/most-black-teenagers-say-racism-has-little-effect-on-day-to
-day-lives.

xix   Dean Baquet quote: "Executive Editor of the NYT: The Left
      Doesn't Want to Hear Thoughtful Disagreement," YouTube
      video, 1:39, posted by NTK Network, May 31, 2017, https://
      www.youtu.be.com/AEUHdOx-DE.

xx    Orlando Patterson quote: Orlando Patterson, "Op-Ed; Race,
      Gender and Liberal Fallacies," *New York Times*, October 21,
      1991,   https://www.nytimes.com/1991/10/20/opinion/op-ed
      -race-gender-and-liberal-fallacies.html.

**INTRODUCTION**

4     Kelly Miller, "Miller Tells Why Roosevelt Deserves Support of
      Race," *Pittsburgh Courier*, March 21, 1936.

6     Janelle Jones, John Schmitt, and Valerie Wilson, "50 Years After
      the Kerner Commission: African Americans are better off in
      many ways but are still disadvantaged by racial inequality,"
      Economic Policy Institute, https://www.epi.org/publication/50
      -years-after-the-kerner-commission/.

**2: ON FAMILY**

45    "Conservatives, Black Lives Matter, Racism," Larry Elder inter-
      view with Scott Rubin on *The Rubin Report*, YouTube video,
      posted by *The Rubin Report*, January 15, 2016, https://www
      .youtu.be.com/IFqVNPwsLNo.

48    "Slave Marriages, Families Were Often Shattered by Auction
      Block," Michel Martin interview with Dr. Tera Hunter on
      NPR's *Tell Me More*, February 11, 2010, https://www.npr.org
      /templates/story/story.php?storyId=123608207.

51    "Statistical Abstract of the United States: 1964," United States
      Census Bureau, July 1964, https://www2.census.gov/library
      /publications/1964/compendia/statab/85ed/1964-02.pdf.

53    On children raised by single mothers: Isabel V. Sawhill, "Are Children Raised with Absent Fathers Worse Off?" Brookings Institution, July 15, 2014, https://www.brookings.edu /opinions/are-children-raised-with-absent-fathers-worse-off/.

54    On welfare and the family: Kay Coles James, "Why We Must Be Bold on Welfare Reform," Heritage Foundation, May 12, 2018, https://www.heritage.org/welfare/commentary/why-we -must-be-bold-welfare-reform.

58    Daniel Patrick Moynihan, "The Negro Family: The Case for National Action," Office of Policy Planning and Research, United States Department of Labor, March 1965, https://web .stanford.edu/~mrosenfe/Moynihan's%20The%20Negro%20 Family.pdf.

59    John J. Conley, "Margaret Sanger was a eugenicist. Why are we still celebrating her?" *America: The Jesuit Review*, November 27, 2017, https://www.americamagazine.org/politics-society/2017/11/27 /margaret-sanger-was-eugenicist-why-are-we-still-celebrating-her.

60    Quotes on sterilization: Margaret Sanger, "My Way to Peace," speech delivered January 17, 1932, https://www.nyu.edu /projects/sanger/webedition   /app/documents/show.php?sanger -Doc=129037.xml.

61    CDC abortion statistics: "Abortion Surveillance—United States, 2016," Centers for Disease Control and Prevention surveillance summaries, November 29, 2019, https://www.cdc .gov/mmwr/volumes/68 /ss/ss6811a1.htm.

62    Life Issues Institute data: Paige Winfield Cunningham, " 'Black babies matter': The black anti-abortion movement's political problem," *Washington Examiner*, September 28, 2015, https:// www.washingtonexaminer.com/black-babies-matter-the-black -anti-abortion-movements-political-problems.

62    https://www.pewsocialtrends.org/2012/11/29/u-s-birth-rate -falls-to-a-record-low-decline-is-greatest-among-immigrants/3/.

62    Rev. Dr. Luke Bobo quote: John Eligon, "When 'Black Lives

Matter' Is Invoked in the Abortion Debate," *New York Times*, July 6, 2019, https://www.nytimes.com/2019/07/06/us/black -abortion-missouri.html.

## 3: ON FEMINISM

68 *New York Times*: "Trump Announces Brett Kavanaugh as Supreme Court Nominee: Full Video and Transcript," *New York Times*, July 10, 2018, https://www.nytimes.com/2018/07/09 /us/politics/trump-supreme-court-announcement-transcript .html.

69 *Politico:* "Full Transcript: Christine Blasey Ford's Opening Statement to the Senate Judiciary Committee," *Politico*, September 26, 2018, https://www.politico.com/story/2018/09/26 /christine-blasey-ford-opening-statement-senate-845080.

69 Burgess Everett, "Woman Denies Attending Party Where Alleged Kavanaugh Assault Occurred," *Politico*, September 23, 2018, https://www.politico.com/story/2018/09/22/kavanaugh -ford-woman-party-letter-836913.

70 Isaac Stanley-Becker, "Christine Blasey Ford's Lawyer Debra Katz: The Feared Attorney of the #MeToo Moment," Washington Post.com, September 24, 2018, https://www.washingtonpost .com/news/morning-mix/wp/2018/09/24/meet-christine -blasey-fords-lawyer-debra-katz-nerves-of-steel-and-proud-to-be -among-the-top-10-plantiffs-attorneys-to-fear-most/.

72 "Help Christine Blasey Ford Organized by Team Christine Blasey Ford," gofundme.com, September 18, 2018, https:// www.gofundme.com/help-christine-blasey-ford.

76 Timothy Tyson, *The Blood of Emmett Till* (New York: Simon & Schuster, 2017).

78 Chris Irvine, "New York Woman, 20, Who Lied about Rapes, Appears to Roll Her Eyes in Court as She's Jailed for a Year," Fox News, August 24, 2018, https://www.foxnews.com/us /new-york-woman-20-who-lied-about-rapes-appears-to-roll -her-eyes-in-court-as-shes-jailed-for-a-year.

79      Harvey and Klein: Enjoli Francis and Bill Hutchinson, "'I don't forgive this woman, and she needs help': Black child wrongly accused of grabbing 'Cornerstore Caroline,'" ABC News.com, October 16, 2018, https://abcnews.go.com/US /white-woman-apologizes-alleging-black-child-assaulted-york /story ?id=58505763.

83      Felton quote: "Biography: FELTON, Rebecca Latimer," History, Art & Archives, United States House of Representatives, https://history.house.gov/People/Listing/F/FELTON,-Rebecca -Latimer-(F000069)/.

84      Jane Fonda: Alanna Vagianos, "Jane Fonda: People Are Listening Now Because Weinstein Victims Are 'Famous and White,'" *Huffington Post*, includes clip of video from MSNBC's *All In with Chris Hayes*, October 26, 2017, https://www.huff post.com/entry /jane-fonda-people-are-listening-now-because -weinstein-victims-are-famous-and-white_n_59f1e023e4 b043885915a337.

## 4: ON OVERCIVILIZATION

88      Transcript, "Ruby Bridges: A Class of One," *PBS NewsHour*, aired on February 18, 1997, https://civilrightsandwrongs.wee -bly.com/uploads/2/6/0/0/26007052/ruby_bridges_a_class _of_one_pbs_newshour_feb.pdf.

89      Williams 2018: Kristen Bayrakdarian, "BSU holds town hall exploring affinity housing," *Williams Record* (Williams College), November 14, 2018, https://williamsrecord.com/2018/11 /bsu-holds-town-hall-exploring-affinity-housing/.

90      Williams 2019: *Williams Record* editorial board, "On the need for affinity housing," *Williams Record*, April 17, 2019, https://williamsrecord.com/2019/04/on-the-need-for -affinity-housing/.

92      Aryn Baker, "Inside the Modern Slave Trade Trapping African Migrants," *Time*, March 14, 2019, https://time.com/long form/african-slave-trade/.

92    *The Economist*, "White Magic: The killing of albinos is over-shadowing Malawi's election," May 11, 2019, https://www.economist.com/middle-east-and-africa/2019/05/11/the-killing-of-albinos-is-overshadowing-malawis-election.

96    Christopher Brito, "Girl admits to lying about sixth grade classmates cutting off her dreadlocks," CBS News, October 1, 2019, https://www.cbsnews.com/news/girl-dreadlocks-lied-classmates-boy-virginia-hairstyle-hoax/.

99    Tom Ascol, "The Cautionary Tale of Amari Allen," Founders Ministries, October 3, 2019, https://founders.org/2019/10/03/the-cautionary-tale-of-amari-allen/.

101   Cristobal de Brey, Lauren Musu, Joel MacFarland, Sidney Wilkinson-Flicker, Melissa Diliberti, Anlan Zhang, Claire Branstetter, and Xialoei Wang, "Status and Trends in the Education of Racial and Ethnic Groups 2018," U.S. Department of Education, National Center for Education Statistics, February 2019, https://nces.ed.gov/pubs2019/2019038.pdf.

## 5: ON SOCIALISM AND GOVERNMENT HANDOUTS

110   Franklin D. Roosevelt, statement on the National Industrial Recovery Act, June 16, 1933, http://docs.fdrlibrary.marist.edu/odnirast.html.

111   Sowell, Thomas, *Economic Facts and Fallacies* (New York: Basic Books, 2008) p. 9.

114   Frank Newport, "Democrats More Positive About Socialism Than Capitalism," Gallup News, August 13, 2018, https://news.gallup.com/poll/240725/democrats-positive-socialism-capitalism.aspx.

115   Karl Marx and Frederick Engels, *Manifesto of the Communist Party* (Marx/Engels *Selected Works*, vol. 1, Progress Publishers, Moscow, 1969, pp. 98–137), available here: https://www.marxists.org/archive/marx/works/download/pdf/Manifesto.pdf, p. 24.

119     Donald J. Trump, speech to the United Nations General Assembly, September 19, 2017, transcript hosted by the White House, https://www.whitehouse.gov/briefings-statements/remarks-president-trump-72nd-session-united-nations-general-assembly/.

119     Margaret Thatcher, speech to Conservative Central Council, March 15, 1986, transcript hosted by Margaret Thatcher Foundation, available here: https://www.margaretthatcher.org/document/106348.

121     NYC Community Health Profiles 2015, "Queens Community District 1: Long Island City and Astoria," available here: https://www1.nyc.gov/assets/doh/downloads/pdf/data/2015 chp-qn01.pdf.

122     Alexandria Ocasio-Cortez Twitter feed, tweet on November 13, 2018, https://twitter.com/AOC/status/1062210420830810113.

122     Alexandria Ocasio-Cortez Twitter feed, tweet on November 17, 2018, https://twitter.com/AOC/status/1063837473099456513.

124     Margaret Thatcher interview with Llew Gardner for Thames TV *This Week*, February 5, 1976, transcript hosted by Margaret Thatcher Foundation, https://www.margaretthatcher.org/document/102953.

125     Winston Churchill, *Why I Am a Free Trader* (London, 1905), reprinted in Stead, *Coming Men on Coming Questions* (London, 1905) and Michael Wolff, ed., *Collected Essays of Sir Winston Churchill* (London, 1975, 4 vols.), II, 23.

126     Washington quote taken from Booker T. Washington Papers, National Negro Business League Files, hosted by the United States Library of Congress, http://lcweb2.loc.gov:8081/ammem/amrlhtml/dtnegbus.html.

## 6: ON EDUCATION

135     Thomas Sowell, *Intellectuals and Race* (New York: Basic Books, 2013), pp. 65–67

144    "The Condition of College & Career Readiness 2019," ACT.org, 2019, https://www.act.org/content/dam/act/unsecured/documents/National-CC CR-2019.pdf.

## 7: ON MEDIA

155    Margaret Sullivan, "NBC needs a transparent, external investigation of its failure to air Ronan Farrow's #MeToo reporting," *Washington Post*, November 5, 2019, https://www.washingtonpost.com /lifestyle/nbc-needs-a-transparent-external-investigation-of-its-failure-to-air-ronan-farrows-metoo-reporting/2019/11/05/0c3a9ef8-ffdc-11e9–8501–2a 7123a38c58_story.html.

159    Maya Rhodan, "Why It Matters if Obama Smokes (and Why It Doesn't)," *Time*, June 10, 2015, updated June 11, 2015, https://time.com/3916342 /barack-obama-smoking/.

162    Joshua Zeitz, "What Everyone Gets Wrong About LBJ's Great Society," *Politico Magazine*, January 28, 2018, https://www.politico.com/magazine/story/2018/01/28/lbj-great-society-josh-zeitz-book-216538.

164    Adam Serwer, "Lyndon Johnson was a civil rights hero. But also a racist," MSNBC.com, April 11, 2014, updated April 12, 2014, http://www.msnbc.com/msnbc/lyndon-johnson-civil-rights-racism.

164    Robert Caro, *Master of the Senate* (New York: Vintage Books, 2003).

165    Jack Bernhardt, "Why Lyndon Johnson, a truly awful man, is my political hero," *Guardian*, January 22, 2018, https://www.theguardian.com/commentisfree/2018/jan/22/lyndon-johnson-anniversary-death-awful-man-my-political-hero.

166    Biden calls Byrd a mentor: Michael McAuliff, "Joe Biden Mourns Byrd," *New York Daily News*, February 22, 2013, https://www.nydailynews.com/blogs /dc/joe-biden-mourns-byrd-blog-entry-1.1661734.

168    Black Lives Matter donation: Influence Watch profile on Black Lives Matter, https://www.influence watch.org/movement/black-lives-matter/.

168    Heather Mac Donald, "Hard Data, Hollow Protests," *City Journal*, September 25, 2017, https:// www.city-journal.org /html/hard-data-hollow-pro tests-15458.html.

170    https://www.weather.gov/safety/lightning-fatalities16.

170    https://www.newsweek.com/police-killings-unarmed-black -men-538542.

171    Interview with Joseph Cesario in reference to "The Truth Behind Racial Disparities in Fatal Police Shootings," *MSU Today* (Michigan State University), July 22, 2019, https://msutoday.msu.edu /news/2019/the-truth-behind-racial-disparities-in-fatal-police -shootings. Full report available at https://www.pnas.org /content/116/32/15877.

## 8: ON EXCUSES

184    Dr. Ben Carson, M.D., *Gifted Hands: The Ben Carson Story* (Zondervan, 1990).

189    "Tyler Perry Gives Powerful Speech of Motivation as He Accepts Ultimate Icon Award," BET Awards 2019, YouTube video, 3:45, posted by BET Networks, June 23, 2019, https:// www.youtu.be.com /DVjjSxpqbOo/.

192    Jessica Semega, Melissa Kollar, John Creamer, and Abinash Mohanty, "Income and Poverty in the United States: 2018," United States Census Bureau, September 2019, https://www.census .gov/content/dam/Census/library/publications/2019/demo /p60–266.pdf.

## 9: ON FAITH

202    Dr. Martin L. King, speech delivered at the March on Washington for Jobs and Freedom, August 28, 1963, transcript available here: https://kinginstitute.stanford.edu/king-papers /documents/i-have-dream-address-delivered-march-washington -jobs-and-freedom.

204    Shelby Steele, *White Guilt* (New York: HarperCollins, 2006), p. 34.

207    Karl Marx, "A Contribution to the Critique of Hegel's Philosophy of Right," available here: https://www.marxists.org /archive/marx/works/1843/critique-hpr/intro.htm.

208    Bible, English Standard Version, Matthew 24: 4–7.

209    Pew Research Center, Religious Landscape Study (RLS-II), May 30, 2014. Study found here: https://www.pewforum.org /wp-content/uploads/sites/7/2015/11/201.11.03_rls_ii_ques -tionnaire.pdf. Results published here: https://www.pewforum .org/religious-landscape-study/christians/christian/.

210    Gallup "In Depth: Topics A to Z: Religion," https://news .gallup.com/poll/1690/religion.aspx.

210    Pew Research Center, "In U.S., Decline of Christianity Continues at Rapid Pace," https://www.pewforum.org/2019/10/17 /in-u-s-decline-of-christianity-continues-at-rapid-pace/.

210    Pew Research Center, Religious Landscape Study (RLS-II), May 30, 2014. Data on "blacks" here: https://www.pewforum .org/religious-landscape-study/racial-and-ethnic-composition /black/.

211    Jeffrey Jones, "U.S. Church Membership Down Sharply in Past Two Decades," Gallup News, April 18, 2019, https://news .gallup.com/poll/248837/church-membership-down-sharply -past-two-decades.aspx.

212    Statement at https://secular.org/wp-content/uploads/2019/08 /DNC-Resolution-on-the-Nonreligious-Demographic.pdf.

214    Catie Edmondson, " 'So Help Me God' No More: Democrats Give House Traditions a Makeover," New York Times, May 11, 2019, https://www.nytimes.com/2019/05/11/us/politics /democrats-house-oath.html.

216    Bible, English Standard Version, Isaiah 2:12.

216    Ibid., Proverbs 13:10.

216    Ibid., Galatians 5:1.

217    Ibid., Lamentations 2:14.

218    Ibid., Matthew 7:15.

218    Ibid., Matthew 23:23–34.

220 Dr. Martin Luther King, speech delivered at Bishop Charles Mason Temple, April 3, 1968, transcript available here: https://kinginstitute.stanford.edu/king-papers/documents /ive-been-mountaintop-address-delivered-bishop-charles -mason-temple.

## 10: On Culture

221 Confucius, *Art of Quotation*, 10 Nov. 2015, artofquotation .wordpress.com/2015/07/26/if-one-should-desire-to-know -whether-a-kingdom-is-well-governed-if-its-morals-are-good -or-bad-the-quality-of-its-music-will-furnish-the-answer -confucius/.

222 The Temptations, "My Girl," Smokey Robinson and Ronald White, Motown Records, December 12, 1964.

222 Megan Thee Stallion, "Savage," Megan Pete, Anthony White, and Bobby Session, Jr., 1501 Certified and 300 Warner, April 7, 2020.

224 Beyoncé, "Formation," *Lemonade*, Parkwood Entertainment, 2016.

224 "Hillary Clinton Interview at The Breakfast Club Power 105.1," YouTube Video, posted by *The Breakfast Club,* April 18, 2016, https://www.youtube.com/watch?v=oRZd861Pog0.

225 "Joe Biden on Black Woman Running Mate, Democrats Taking Black Voters for Granted + Wiping Weed Crime," YouTube Video, Posted by *The Breakfast Club*, May 22, 2020, https:// www.youtube.com/watch?v=KOIFs_SryHI.

226 Eric Levitz, "Will Black Voters Still Love Biden When They Remember Who He Was?," *New York Magazine*, March 12, 2019, https://nymag.com/intelligencer/2019/03 /joe-biden-record-on-busing-incarceration-racial-justice -democratic-primary-2020-explained.html.

228 Bible, English Standard Version, 1 John 5:21.

228 Ibid., Leviticus 19:4.

228 Ibid., Psalm 16:4.

230 Bill Strande, "Transcript of 911 call on George Floyd released,"

KARE 11, May 28, 2020, https://www.kare11.com/article
/news/local/george-floyd/transcript-of-911-call-on-george-floyd
-is-released/89-34f18837-3b09-421b-b3db-e2c0f5dfa6fa.

230    Eliott McLaughlin, "Three videos piece together the final moments of George Floyd's life," CNN, June 1, 2020, https://
www.cnn.com/2020/06/01/us/george-floyd-three-videos
-minneapolis/index.html.

232    "Sharpton at George Floyd memorial: 'Get your knee off our
necks,'" YouTube Video, Posted by *The Los Angeles Times*, June
4, 2020, https://www.youtube.com/watch?v=gEghWqk_F9k.

233    "Arrest in fatal shooting of beloved retired St. Louis police captain during protests," CBS News, June 8, 2020, https://www
.cbsnews.com/news/david-dorn-arrest-suspect-killing-st-louis
-police-captain-protest/.

233    FBI: Uniform Crime Report, "Table 29: Estimated Number
of Arrests," https://ucr.fbi.gov/crime-in-the-u.s/2018/crime-in
-the-u.s.-2018/tables/table-29.

233    "Police Shooting Database 2015–2020," *The Washington Post*,
June 9, 2020, https://www.washingtonpost.com/graphics
/investigations/police-shootings-database/.

233    Sachin Jangra, "George Floyd Criminal Past Record of Arrest
History/Career Timeline: Robbery, Baggie, Gun Pregnant and
All Details," *The Courier Daily*, June 6, 2020, https://thecourier
-daily.com/george-floyd-criminal-past-record-arrest/20177/.

235    Daniel Villarreal, "George Floyd Was on Fentanyl, Medical Examiner Says, As Experts Dispute Cause of Death," *Newsweek*, June
2, 2020, https://www.newsweek.com/george-floyd-was-fentanyl
-medical-examiner-says-experts-dispute-cause-death-1507982.

236    Heather Mac Donald, "The Myth of Systemic Police Racism,"
*Wall Street Journal*, June 2, 2020, https://www.wsj.com/articles
/the-myth-of-systemic-police-racism-11591119883.

## 11: ON SLAVERY

239    Ginger Gibson, "Senator Elizabeth Warren backs reparations

for black Americans," February 21, 2019, https://www .reuters.com/article/us-usa-election-warren/senator-elizabeth -warren-backs-reparations-for-black-americans-idUSKCN 1QA2WF.

240    CNN Newsroom, Transcripts, February 26, 2019, "Some 2020 Candidates Back Idea of Slavery Reparations," http:// transcripts.cnn.com/TRANSCRIPTS/1902/26/cnr.08. html.

240    Juana Summers, AP News, "O'Rourke, Castro talk reparations at civil rights conference," April 3, 2019, https://apnews.com /ffa90003022044a288cc0cd1a54f3eaf.

242    *Times of Israel* staff, "World War III trends on social media following Soleimani killing," January 5, 2020, https://www .timesofisrael.com/world-war-iii-trends-on-social-media -following-soleimani-killing/.

242    Sophie Lewis, CBS News, "Rose McGowan defends tweet apologizing to Iran after airstrike," January 4, 2020, https://www .cbsnews.com/news/rose-mcgowan-iran-actress-defends-tweet -apologizing-to-iran-after-airstrike-kills-qassem-soleimani/.

243    Human Rights Watch, "Women's Rights in Iran," October 28, 2015, https://www.hrw.org/news/2015/10/28/womens-rights -iran.

245    Hank Berrien, "Kaepernick Quotes Frederick Douglass to Bash July 4th. Cruz Crushes Him with Facts," *Daily Wire News*, July 5, 2019, https://www.dailywire.com/news/kaepernick-quotes -frederick-douglass-bash-july-4th-hank-berrien.

246    Rodney Stark, *How the West Won* (Wilmington, DE: Intercollegiate Studies Institute, 2015), pp. 221–22.

247    John Noble Wilford, "New Data Suggests Some Cannibalism by Ancient Indians," *New York Times*, September 7, 2000, https:// www.nytimes.com/2000/09/07/us/new-data-suggests-some -cannibalism-by-ancient-indians.html.

250    Thomas Hobbes, *Of Man: Leviathan*, 1651 (New York: P. F. Collier, 1909–14).

252     Leif Coorlim, "Child slaves risk their lives on Ghana's Lake Volta," CNN, February 2019, https://edition.cnn.com/interactive/2019/02/africa/ghana-child-slaves-intl/.

254     Tyler D. Parry, "How the 'Democratic Plantation' became one of conservatives' favorite slurs," *Washington Post*, January 8, 2019, https://www.washingtonpost.com/outlook/2019/01/08/how-democratic-plantation-became-one-conservatives-favorite-slurs/.

257     Frederick Douglass, *Narrative of the Life of Frederick Douglass* (Boston: Anti-Slavery Office, 1845), pp. 2–4.

259     Plato, *Republic*, VII, "The Allegory of the Cave" (translation by Thomas Sheehan), https://web.stanford.edu/class/ihum40/cave.pdf.

266     Emily Rolen and Brian Hickey, "ANTIFA protesters confront conservative activists Charlie Kirk, Candace Owens at Philly Restaurant," August 6, 2018, https://www.phillyvoice.com/antifa-protesters-charlie-kirk-candance-owens-philly-restaurant-turning-point-usa/.

267     Joe Concha, "CNN's Cuomo defends Antifa: Those who oppose hate 'are on the side of right,'" *The Hill*, August, 14, 2018, https://thehill.com/homenews/media/401699-cnns-cuomo-defends-antifa-those-who-oppose-hate-are-on-the-side-of-right.

267     "Senators Question Clarence Thomas," C-SPAN clip, October 11, 1991, https://www.c-span.org/video/?c4763224/user-clip-thomas-high-tech-lynching.

## CONCLUSION

275     Matt Bruenig and Ryan Cooper, "How Obama Destroyed Black Wealth," *Jacobin Magazine*, December 7, 2017, https://jacobinmag.com/2017/12/obama-foreclosure-crisis-wealth-inequality.

281     President Donald J. Trump Inaugural Address: https://www.whitehouse.gov/briefings-statements/the-inaugural-address/.

## ACKNOWLEDGMENTS

A book is a labor of love and a testament to the proverb that it takes a village.

First, I would like to thank to my grandfather. Thank you for the courage that it took to live through all that you did—with morality, faith, and love.

To my siblings, Ashlee, Brittany, and Dante: we broke the cycle. I am proud of us every single day for choosing something different from our upbringing. To my cousin Kymia, thank you for consistently reminding me of who I am and who I never have to be.

To my husband, George, for standing by my side every

day. For choosing me, for loving me, and for your faith in me and this completely uncharted course that we are on.

Thank you to my creative director, Jesse Grainger, for always believing in my vision, even when no one else did.

Finally, to the whole team at Threshold Editions, including Jennifer Long, associate publisher; and most important, to Natasha Simons, my rock-star editor; Natasha, you have a heart of gold, and I will forever be grateful for your kindness and graciousness.

God bless you all. . . . And here's to a 2020 Blackout!